Analytic Writing Guide

Louis M. Kaiser
Randolph H. Pherson

Pherson Associates, LLC
1892 Preston White Drive
Suite 300
Reston, Virginia 20191
www.pherson.org

Analytic Writing Guide

Copyright 2014, Pherson Associates, LLC.

Reprinted 2017

All rights reserved. No part of this publication may be reproduced or utilized in any form by any means, electronic or mechanical, including photocopying, recording, or by any information storage and retrieval system, without express written permission from the publisher.

ISBN-13: 978-0-9798880-2-1
ISBN-10: 0979888026

Managing Editor: Kristen M. Reynolds

Cover Design: Nigah M. Ajaj and Kristen M. Reynolds

Photography: Randolph H. Pherson

Author Photographer: Brooke Bready

Marketing Manager: Cynthia M. Jensen

Proofreading Symbols Glossary: GEMI, Inc.

Printed in the United States of America

Table of Contents

Preface i

About the Authors iii

Part I: Improving Your Writing 1

1. Practice, Practice, Practice 3

Part II: Organizing the Analysis 7

2. Create a Mission Statement 9
3. Develop an Analytic Line of March 13
4. Prepare a Detailed Outline 21

Part III: Writing the First Draft 27

5. Build Paragraphs Around Good Topic Sentences 29
6. Answer All Likely Questions 41
7. Order the Supporting Information 49
8. Treat Peripheral Information Separately 57

Part IV: Refining the Draft 61

9. Review Paragraphs for Analytic Coherence 63
10. Economize on Words 67
11. Conduct a Final Review 71

Glossaries 77

A. Commonly Used Terms 79

B. Proofreading Symbols 83

C. Recommended Readings 85

Preface

Why This Book?

Who has not submitted a paper for review and had it come back with the white spaces filled with comments, edits, and rewrites? This guide is aimed primarily at authors who want to learn how to write better and avoid such experiences. Reviewers of analytic papers also may find the guide a useful tool for developing the skill of writers under their charge.

The guidelines are intended as an alternative to the all-too-common practice where reviewers rework drafts based on a largely internalized set of standards and return edited drafts without a lot of explanation. Two corollaries to this approach are the "I-will-know-it-when-I-see-it" litmus test for reviewing a paper and the "draft meets the threshold for publication because it satisfies everything on the good writing checklist." These macro-level approaches to analytic writing usually do not help the drafter identify what he or she could have done to improve the paper before it went to the reviewer.

Analysts, students, law enforcement officers, policymakers, and business executives are the primary target audience for this book, but the principles underlying the teaching points are applicable to anyone seeking to communicate ideas more effectively—including high school and university students. The details and specifics in the examples are fictitious, but the underlying writing problems they reflect are all too real.

Content and Design

This guide explains the underlying rationale for why language should be moved, deleted, or added. We organized the answers to these questions into ten chapters, each with a tailored set of guidelines for easy access. The guidelines will improve your drafts but will not prevent your work from being edited. The role of reviewers is to make your paper clearer and easier to read; they will make revisions even if you apply these guidelines faithfully. However, you and the reviewers will benefit because they can track your conclusions more easily and follow your line of argument.

Material in tan-shaded boxes expands upon some of the key concepts presented in the writing guidelines. Purple-shaded boxes provide specific examples that illustrate the various teaching points in the text. Sentences excerpted from the narrative are interspersed throughout the text in **purple** ink to underscore key points.

Photographs appear throughout the text to illustrate core writing concepts that often employ architectural terms such as steps, bridges, pillars, and cornerstones. The pictures were taken by Randolph H. Pherson during a visit to **Toledo, Spain** in February 2013 that included a tour of the Toledo Army Museum. Toledo is a UNESCO World Heritage site and home of Miguel de Cervantes, author of Don Quixote—a book that captures many of the frustrations writers encounter when they deal with editors. In lieu of providing captions for each photograph, the relevant portion of text is highlighted in **purple**.

Acknowledgments

Mr. Kaiser would like to thank the students in the Career Analyst Program of the Central Intelligence Agency (CIA), whom he had the great pleasure to get to know and who challenged him daily. The origins of this book began with all the questions the students raised. Both authors would like to thank Katherine Pherson and Mary O'Sullivan, who helped us conceptualize and organize the book; Alysa Gander, Stephanie Gleason, William Johnson, Susan Oliver, Katherine Pherson, Richard Pherson, Erv Rokke, and Cynthia Storer, who helped review, edit, and proof the text; and Nigah Ajaj and Amanda Pherson, who provided graphics support and helped design the cover. In addition, we are indebted to Kristen Reynolds, our managing editor, who formatted the book, oversaw creative direction, and managed its production.

All statements of fact, opinion, or analysis expressed in this book are those of the authors and do not reflect the official positions of the Office of the Director on National Intelligence (ODNI), the CIA, or any other US Government agency. Nothing in the text should be construed as asserting or implying the authentication of information or the endorsement of the authors' views by the US Government. This material has been reviewed by the ODNI and the CIA only to prevent the disclosure of classified material.

About the Authors

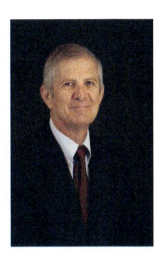

Louis M. Kaiser, an associate of Pherson Associates, LLC, retired from the Central Intelligence Agency (CIA) after 30 years of service in the Directorate of Intelligence (DI) where he mastered the art of analytic writing. He has more than 10 years of experience in mentoring and teaching new and junior analysts in intelligence tradecraft and writing, including a four-year stint with the DI's Sherman Kent School of Intelligence Analysis. He served as an editor for three separate DI publications, was a member of the Senior Analytic Service, and was awarded the Career Intelligence Medal. Mr. Kaiser received a B.S. in Mining Engineering from Virginia Polytechnic Institute and State University, a M.S. in Operations Research and Management Science from George Mason University, and an M.A. in European History from Catholic University.

Randolph H. Pherson, President of Pherson Associates, LLC and CEO of Globalytica, LLC, teaches advanced analytic techniques and critical thinking skills to analysts in the government and private sector. He authored *The Handbook of Analytic Tools and Techniques* and co-authored *Structured Analytic Techniques for Intelligence Analysis* with Richards J. Heuer, Jr.; *Cases in Intelligence Analysis: Structured Analytic Techniques in Action* with Sarah Miller Beebe; and *Critical Thinking for Strategic Intelligence* with Katherine Hibbs Pherson. Mr. Pherson completed a 28-year career in the Intelligence Community in 2000, last serving as National Intelligence Officer (NIO) for Latin America. Previously, at the CIA, Mr. Pherson managed the production of intelligence analysis on topics ranging from global instability to Latin America, served on the Inspector General's staff, and was Chief of the CIA's Strategic Planning and Management Staff. He is the recipient of the Distinguished Intelligence Medal for his service as NIO and the Distinguished Career Intelligence Medal. Mr. Pherson received his B.A. from Dartmouth College and an M.A. in International Relations from Yale University.

Part I: Improving Your Writing

This book is a user's guide for writing papers, short memos, and emails when the objective is to inform a busy reader inundated with other papers and preoccupied with other tasks. It focuses on ideas and information: making sure that all the information needed to understand the main points is in the paper and in the right order, minimizing or eliminating extraneous information and ideas, and resolving inconsistencies. The guide offers a mix of strategic and tactical advice, ranging from how to get started to how to order information in a paragraph.

The recommendations we provide are not hard-and-fast rules, but general guidelines. Every paper is a unique undertaking that requires its own approach. You as the author are the ultimate judge—at least initially, before you pass your paper forward for review—of which principles apply to your paper and which do not.

This is not a book about grammar; nor is it a treatise on critical thinking. Grammar and style are undeniably important, but elegantly written sentences will fail to communicate your conclusions if the flow of ideas and information is flawed. If your reader has difficulty understanding the relationship between your ideas and information, you have no hope of persuading your target audience to accept your conclusions. If the flow of ideas and information is muddled, your reader will seldom read the paper in its entirety.

In a well-written paper, the ideas and information are presented so that the paper has a certain momentum and rhythm—it should have a succinct message and tell a convincing story. The objective is to ensure that the reader does not get lost or become impatient, but moves quickly through the paper to its final paragraph. The **path** should be straightforward, with the primary objective always in sight for the reader. This guide is designed to help you in that endeavor. In Part I, we will discuss the value of:

Practice, Practice, Practice

1. Practice, Practice, Practice

Writing analytic papers is an acquired skill, with the emphasis on "acquired." This skill will take time to develop with a lot of hard work and purposeful attention to specific tasks and skill sets. Analytic writing must convey a message rather than merely describe a situation or an incident. Presenting a message that gets your customers' attention, interest, and trust is all about conveying your analytic conclusions with clarity, precision, and brevity. What is the value your busy customer will get from reading the piece? What is the value the taxpayer or your company gets from having you research and write it?

Ultimately, the value depends on how well you convey your thoughts and conclusions on paper. Brilliant analysis that is poorly conveyed is not useful because the reader will be confused about the message and uncertain about what to do or think as a result of the analysis. If the intent is to convey a compelling message or analysis, then efficient, effective writing is essential.[1]

The basic precepts are easy to grasp. If you can establish a set of benchmarks to organize your flow of ideas and information based on your reader's needs, your paper will be tightly focused. Include only that information that is key to supporting the main points of your analysis (see Figure 1). The fundamental task in an analytic paper is to present ideas and information in a way that enables the target audience to process your information and conclusions quickly.

---

[1] For guidance on how best to accomplish these tasks see Pherson and Pherson, *Critical Thinking for Strategic Intelligence,* Chapters 16 and 19: Is My Argument Persuasive? and How Do I Present My Message in the Most Compelling Way?, pp. 179 and 211.

Figure 1. Nine Principles of Effective Analytic Writing

1. **Determine the context and put conclusions first.** Determine the big picture and put the conclusions up front; begin with judgments and then support them.

2. **Know the customer's needs.** Customers look for insights and judgments that will help them make decisions as well as warnings about matters that might require action.

3. **Organize logically.** Present the conclusions in a logical and orderly way to avoid confusing the reader and introducing redundancy.

4. **Understand formats.** Each publication, including memos and emails, has its own structural design that helps you organize your information.

5. **Use precise language.** Everyone who reads what you have written should come away with the same message.

6. **Economize on words.** Seek brevity and succinctness in your writing. Use clear, familiar, and simple terms. Make each word count.

7. **Strive for clarity of thought.** Remember that writing is thinking on paper. When the meaning of your writing is not clear, the thoughts behind your words may not be clear.

8. **Use active voice.** Active voice makes your writing more direct, vigorous, and concise.

9. **Self-edit your writing.** Self-edit your work or ask a colleague to check your draft before you submit it for review. Avoid grammatical and typographical errors.

Strive to become known as someone who is a superb writer. The characterization often used to describe a poor writer is akin to a summary judicial decision: he cannot write, end of story. This characterization has an aura of finality about it, and can become a self-fulfilling prophecy. The phrase "he cannot write" is so ambiguous that the proper response is: "What do you mean, exactly?" Most of the time, the response will have nothing to do with "writing" and everything to do with a flawed presentation of ideas and information.

The rationale for moving, deleting, or adding text is more about logic and thinking than grammar, vocabulary, or literary flow. You do not need to have majored in English or have been a voracious reader to be a good writer. What you do need, however, is a set of guidelines that help you optimize the flow of ideas and information so your readers can follow your argument without wondering why you believe what you believe, or, worse, wondering what you are trying to convey in the first place.

As for grammar, lean on your editor. A good editor can quickly review a well-constructed draft, fixing grammatical mistakes and improving it stylistically. A draft that is not well thought out is a challenge to edit and probably will be returned to the author for more work.

Good writing is good "thinking on paper."[2] If you have thought through your organizational framework, your sources of information, and your argument, then the "writing" will come, maybe not easily but eventually. If all the necessary information is there, eventually you will be able to arrange this information so that a clear and convincing message appears. If your paper is missing critical bits of information to support your argument, your most important task is to fill these gaps with additional information, well-supported assumptions, or solid logic.

Analytic writing should be one of the easier forms of writing to master. The emphasis in analytic writing is more on the analysis and clarity of thought than on literary writing. If a reader can reconstruct the basis for your conclusions, you can craft effective analytic papers. Literary writing has many complex techniques and forms that appear intended to make the reader's work harder, not easier.

Devising these clever constructions is an undertaking in itself. In some forms of literary writing, the meaning is deliberately hidden among the words. In analytic writing, the last thing you want to do is to hide behind the words. If your judgments and the basis for those judgments are muddled, your chances of writing an effective analytic paper are diminished.

Regardless of how good a writer you think you are, editors will always make changes to your text. Even well-written papers are frequently revised with significant editorial changes. Some editors are better than others. When you find really skilled editors, pay close attention to their suggested changes. If you can ask yourself what prompted them to add, move, or delete text, you will learn something. If you do not understand why a change was made, ask the editor to explain. Make those teaching points part of your "writing consciousness" that you draw upon the next time you write a paper.

---

[2] For guidance on how best to accomplish these tasks see Pherson and Pherson, *Critical Thinking for Strategic Intelligence,* Chapters 4, 5, 9, and 12: How Should I Conceptualize My Product?, What is My Analytic Approach?, Can I Trust the Sources?, and Can I Make My Case?, pp. 35, 43, 97, and 129.

This handbook provides a number of guidelines for arranging your ideas and information, but it is by no means exhaustive. When you begin drafting, one of the first questions to ask yourself is: "What type of product am I writing?" Data-driven products are more likely to summarize and generalize while concept-driven papers are more likely to judge, evaluate, and forecast. Recognizing the appropriate framework for your product makes it much easier to write (see Figure 2 on page 6).[3]

Progress in improving your writing may be slow at first, but it will get faster the more you work at it. Be patient; it can take years to learn how to be an expert writer. When you add, delete, or move text, and the result is a structural improvement in the flow of ideas and information, make a mental note of what you did and exactly why you did it. Better yet, record your own list of observations in a notebook. This will create a more lasting impression than a brief mental note. Organize these observations so that you can refer to them easily. For example, what sentence construction, arrangement of information in a paragraph, or paper organization struck you as particularly well done. Note how these exemplars made the presentation of ideas and information more effective.

Progress in improving your writing may be slow at first, but it will get faster the more you work at it. Be patient; it can take years to learn how to be an expert writer.

Invest your time in reviewing papers written by others. When you find a paper that is particularly well crafted, study it to identify new guidelines that you can add to your list. Just as important, when you find text in someone else's paper that is not clear, ask yourself why and what can be done to clarify the point. Over time, you will internalize a set of self-editing guidelines that will enable you to rearrange text as fast as or faster than you can identify the reason for the change. Your work will still be edited, but your analytic abilities will shine and edited drafts will be returned to you more quickly.

---

[3] A more detailed discussion of the categories of analytic products that comprise The Analytic Spectrum can be found in Pherson and Pherson, *Critical Thinking for Strategic Intelligence*, Chapter 5: What is My Analytic Approach, p. 43.

Figure 2. Types of Analytic Products

Analytic products can be divided into five broad types. Knowing which category a paper falls into makes it easier to write.

Basic information is reference material. For example: *How large is the port?*
- Primary goal: To describe, e.g., <u>CIA World Factbook</u> or <u>Foreign Investment Regulations in China</u>.
- It is factual information or the baseline knowledge on a subject that provides context, is often updated, and periodically updated.
- Answers the **"What?"** question.

Current reports focus on new developments. For example: *How many ships arrived today?*
- Primary goal: To inform or explain, e.g., <u>Market Penetration Opportunities in the Maritime Sector</u>.
- A daily digest of events, situation report (*sitrep*), or annual survey. It describes what is happening and may provide background information for context and address near-term threats and consequences.
- Answers the **"What?"** and sometimes the **"Why?"** and the **"So What?"** questions.

Evaluative assessments address why a development or event occurred, its implications, and often explore second and third order consequences. For example: *Why are the ships arriving now?*
- Primary goal: To evaluate, e.g., <u>The Growing Threat Posed by Self-Radicalization</u>.
- It provides an analytic framework for understanding the issue, describes the key drivers, puts the issue in context, and often focuses on implications. It may include actionable intelligence.
- Answers the **"So What of the So What?"** question.

Estimative reports judge probable outcomes. For example: *When will the port be full?*
- Primary goal: To forecast or predict, e.g., <u>World Trends in 2020</u>.
- Usually forward-looking, predictive judgments. Often focuses on key drivers, emerging issues, most likely scenarios, and indicators.
- Could be "strategic" (long term trends or patterns) or "tactical" (the adversary's likely next move).

Warning assessments try to anticipate the future. For example: *They are getting ready to attack!*
- Primary goal: To forewarn or sound an alarm, e.g., <u>Military Maneuvers Suggest Preparations for Attack</u>.
- Usually concerns imminent threat or opportunity; predicated on presence of indicators.
- May suggest how threat could be mitigated or opportunity exploited.

Information in this Figure was derived from Pherson and Pherson, <u>Critical Thinking for Strategic Intelligence</u> (2013), and an exercise from the Analytic Writing Course, Intelligence Analyst Learning Program, Government of Canada (2013) and is used with the permission of the Canadian government.

Part II: Organizing the Analysis

The more forethought you give to the analytic issue that is the focus of your paper, the easier and faster it will be to write and the less likely it will end up stuck in a reviewer's inbox. One technique we recommend is to craft a two or three sentence summary of the paper as you start drafting. Revise it as you refine your message during the drafting process. Dedicate time and attention up front to determine the paper's key message for the intended audience, define the major questions and issues that will be addressed in the paper, and assimilate and organize the details.

Consider writing your conclusions early on in the drafting, or even at the beginning. If you understand your subject, you should have a good sense of where you will end up. Writing conclusions early focuses you on the message and is beneficial even if you have to rewrite them.

Timing is critical. A paper that arrives after the meeting is held or the event has occured is wasted effort. Similarly, a paper that is delivered well before the customer is ready to focus on the topic may be ignored. In Part II, we discuss how to:

Create a Mission Statement
Develop an Analytic Line of March
Prepare a Detailed Outline

2. Create a Mission Statement

If you cannot articulate the paper's bottom line in a single sentence or two—the mission statement—you are not ready to write the paper. The authors call this the pre-drafting litmus test. A clear and focused mission statement includes your target audience and the key message for those readers: what it is that they need to know and why do they need to know it? You may not have completed all of your research at this point, but you should have completed enough to identify an analytic message that is important to your target audience (see Figure 3). If you have not, then you are not ready to proceed further because you are aiming blindly and have little chance of producing a paper that is on target for your intended reader. Many papers end up muddled and without a clear focus because they are drafted on the fly, without a mission statement.

Figure 3. The Key First Step: Determine the AIMS of Your Product

- Who is your primary **A**udience?
- What key **I**ssue(s) are those consumers struggling with now or will be dealing with in the near future?
- What is the bottom-line **M**essage you want to convey?
- With the bottom-line message in mind, how can you best present the **S**toryline (or "overall package")?

Think of your paper's mission statement as its analytic bottom line at the pre-drafting stage. It should be short, preferably no more than one sentence, precise, and relevant to the target audience's needs. Your mission statement ideally could serve as the basis for a one-minute briefing.

Envision a situation where the person you were asked to brief must cut the briefing short and asks for the main points as she heads out the door or up the elevator. If you do not know your bottom line, you could find yourself:

- Launching into background details that consume your one minute before you ever get to the main takeaway, explaining how your target audience might be affected.

- Telling a company executive that developments in a certain industry are going to raise the price of a commodity in which her company has little interest.

- Describing to a policymaker what research you have conducted instead of listing the implications of your findings for your country's national interests.

You can increase the odds that analysis will have impact by having a clear, focused message—preferably up front—that is relevant to your readers' needs and useful in helping them meet their objectives. You need to put a lot of thought into your mission statement so it helps you decide which issues you will discuss and which ones you will not. A mission statement also helps you conceptualize the paper's title and organization—the next steps in crafting your paper. It serves as a lens through which you maintain the focus of your draft as you proceed. It is the **keystone** around which the entire argument for the paper is constructed.

Before settling on your mission statement, you should engage in some discussion, brainstorming, and vetting of various directions that your paper could take with your colleagues, managers, and other experts.

You cannot write a good mission statement if you have not thought through all the ramifications of the issues under consideration. You need to consider five possible questions or components for every analytic problem in crafting your mission statement.

- The *"what?"*: The development or event that has occurred.
- The *"why now?"*: The explanation for why the development has occurred now, focusing on the motivations of the main actor(s) in your paper. What are the forces or factors driving the issue?
- The *impact so far*: What has changed because of the development?
- The *"what next?"* or *outlook*: Where the development is likely to go or could go.
- Last, the *implications*: What does it mean for your target audience? Does it help them make better decisions? Does it present opportunities to exploit or dangers to avoid? Does it identify levers the readers can bring to bear to influence an issue? Does it illuminate what one can do, and what will prevent others from acting?

You can increase the odds that your paper is read by having a clear, focused message—preferably up front—that is relevant to your readers' needs and useful in helping them meet their objectives.

Almost all mission statements should include at least two of these five components: either a *"what?"* or *"why now?"* matched with an *impact so far*, *outlook*, or *implications*. These are the **pillars** that support the main argument. In some instances, such as when the focus of your analysis is on an event or development that is likely to occur in the future, you might choose to begin with an *outlook* followed by *implications*. Allow the uniqueness of your message and the circumstances of what your target audience knows and needs to know to shape your mission statement. Think of the *"what?"* section as the information the target audience needs to know and the *implications* section as the explanation of why they need to know it, or the *"so what?"*

Not every paper will require an *outlook* or an *implications* section. In some cases, the discussion of the *outlook* and *implications* may be another paper in itself; delaying the paper until the *outlook* and *implications* are thought through is not advisable. Such papers could "end" with the *impact* section, especially if the *impact so far* has direct consequences, such as when an adversary or competitor is taking action against your country or your organization. For example:

- In 1963, at the height of the Cold War, the Soviet Union placed medium-range ballistic missiles in Cuba, a communist country tied to the Soviet Union. The main focus of this paper might be to convey the basis for the judgment on missiles in Cuba (the *"what?"*) and how much of the United States would be vulnerable given the missiles' range (the *impact so far*).
- Bleakistan has developed a cyber capability (the *"what?"*) that could shut down all banking operations in the United States (the *impact so far*). You may know little about the intent behind the capability; writing a separate paper on how Bleakistan may use this new capability (the *outlook*) might be the best approach.

Papers that "end" with the *impact so far* without going into the *outlook* or *implications* are, for the most part, rare. In the second example above, if the analytic bottom line was that Bleakistan is developing a cyber capability to shut down the banking sector, further discussion in the paper on the prospects and outlook for successful development would be necessary or the analysis would have limited utility.

The mission statement should focus on where your analysis stops because this is typically where your paper has the most relevance for the target audience (see Figure 4). For example, if your analysis continues beyond the *impact so far* and discusses *implications*, your mission statement needs to devote more space to the *implications* and less to other aspects of the issue at hand. Remember, your mission statement is your analytic bottom line. If you had only one minute to convey it, you would craft it so it did not get lost in the details or tangled in a sequence of future events that cloud the main message.

> *The mission statement should focus on where your analysis stops because this is typically where your paper has the most relevance for the target audience.*

Your mission statement is not a cast-in-stone contract; you should modify it as your analysis changes during drafting or as you acquire new information. Without a mission statement, you might easily add irrelevant material or veer off course, ending with analysis that has no clear focus.

Figure 4. Mission Statements That Can Be Improved

Original Sentence	Improved Variant
To inform senior policymakers that political unrest in Bleakistan is likely to increase and have political implications for the United States.	To inform senior policymakers that political unrest in Bleakistan—driven largely by economic considerations—is likely to increase as the economy deteriorates and threatens the government's hold on power.
To inform a business associate that the company's financial position has deteriorated sharply because of a competitor's market inroads.	To inform a business associate that the company's financial position has deteriorated sharply because of a competitor's market inroads, and the company will need to incur additional loans or will not be able to make its scheduled payments on existing loans.
To inform a city supervisor that the proposed budget for the police department will require cuts in police patrols.	To inform a city supervisor that the proposed budget for the police department will require cuts in police patrols and lead to increased crime in certain areas of the city.
To inform your parents that you have decided to attend graduate school but cannot afford the tuition.	To inform your parents that you have decided to attend graduate school and would like them to pay for it because you lack the resources and do not want to take out huge loans.

3. Develop an Analytic Line of March

Before you can begin to prepare an outline, you should establish the paper's general analytic direction based on the five possible focal questions: *"what?", "why now?", impact so far, outlook,* and *implications.* The answers to these questions comprise individual, stand-alone analytic stories within the broader paper. No matter which of the five questions you decide to address, you should maintain the order in which you address these questions in most cases. That order is inherently sound and establishes a baseline of building block knowledge that prepares readers to assimilate key points as you develop the analytic message in the paper's subsequent sections.

What has changed?

The *"what?"* can be a tangible, observable change or new insight based on research; it is where we are today that is new or different from where we were yesterday. Most of the time something has changed; this is typically the initial focus of an analytic paper. The issue that the target audience should most be aware of is the difference between what was and what is now. The target audience has a core interest in the issue and especially the change or new insight concerning the issue. The *"what?"* can be:

- An event or series of events: Troops being moved to the border, a medical breakthrough, or a decline in a stock's price.

- A condition or situation: Political chaos, an economic downturn, a company's financial bottom line, low morale among employees, or reduced deaths from a disease.

- A decision or series of decisions or statements: A president's decision not to run for office again, an employee's decision to sue, or a company's decision to offer a 2-for-1 stock split.

- A view or perception: A country's threat perceptions or the evolving views of the benefits of democracy in another country.

- A societal behavioral norm or pattern: The increased use of narcotics among youth or the expanding role of women in an Arab country.

Most of the time something has changed; this is typically the initial focus of an analytic paper. The issue that the target audience should most be aware of is the difference between what was and what is now.

Why has the change occurred?

The *"why now?"* addresses the factors that generated the *"what?"* It is a critically important analytic question. Whether explicitly stated or implied, the most important word or concept in a *"why now?"* section is "because." Before your target audience can even begin to think about how to improve a situation or take advantage of a potential opportunity, a thorough understanding of the forces and factors underlying the *"what?"* is essential. The *"why now?"* can include:

- The subject's interests and objectives: A whole host of explanations is possible, including, but certainly not limited to, money, security, power, or pride.

- Economic and technological developments: Explanations include macro-economic indices such as unemployment or inflation; narrowly focused developments, such as the rising price of a commodity; or a major breakthrough in a technology.

- Cultural, social, and religious forces: These are some of the most powerful drivers of change, in part because they are deeply rooted and arouse intense sentiment and passion when change occurs. Often they are the most misunderstood by outside observers.

- Historical experience: History may not repeat itself, but neither is it forgotten. The old adage that generals prepare to fight the last war may be one explanation for minor changes in war strategy.

- Personality traits: If you are focusing on specific individuals, explain what emotional make-up and decision making style drives their behavior. Are they daring or timid, vengeful or trusting, thorough planners or prone to act on instinct?

- Group dynamics: Interaction within and between groups may produce drivers that are totally unexpected. Group dynamics as a factor increases in importance particularly when substantial parity exists among groups and members jockey for position and dominance.

- Beliefs and perceptions: These drivers may or may not be based in reality, but they operate as if they are. Beliefs and perceptions create a prism of assumptions and premises through which actors interpret and make sense of others' behaviors, albeit not always accurately.

The *"what?"* in your paper may involve multiple developments occurring simultaneously. For example, a political leader may be consolidating control of his security services while the local media start portraying his leadership in a glowing, almost worshipful tone. If the *"why now?"* applies to both developments, the standard organization of *"what?"*, then *"why now?"* works. If, however, the developments were driven by different factors, it is best to deal with the *"what?"* and *"why now?"* for the first factor, followed by the *"what?"* and *"why now?"* for the second factor because this organization reduces the mental "whipsawing" between different issues. For example, if you have determined that a certain leader's reluctance to engage in peace talks is due to concern over a potential backlash from political rivals inside the country as well as to the leader's dislike of the foreign country pushing for talks, the *"why nows?"* underlying those factors probably are not related. Combining that discussion into one section probably would disrupt the paper's continuity.

The most important word or concept in a "why now?" section is "because." Before your target audience can even begin to think about how to improve a situation or take advantage of a potential opportunity, a thorough understanding of the forces and factors underlying the "what?" is essential.

What is the impact so far?

A stand-alone section that discusses the *impact so far* generally is limited to situations in which the impact is an intermediate result that sets the stage for future developments of a qualitatively different nature. For example, rising unemployment (the *"what?"*) has led to a sharp increase in crime (the *impact so far*) that probably will lead to an increase in gun purchases by individuals concerned about crime and demands for stiffer penalties for violent crimes.

A separate section on impact works nicely when multiple actors are cited. It would allow you to separate what Actor A has done from how Actor B responded. For example, if Freedonia is moving troops to the border because it believes Bleakistan is responsible for a political assassination in Freedonia, an *impact* section would be an appropriate place to discuss Bleakistan's response to Freedonia's troop movements. For papers in which multiple **protagonists** are engaged in a rapid series of actions and reactions; you might not have an *impact* section because the response-counter-response behavior would be the focus of the "*what?*" section.

What is likely to happen next?

Outlook sections that look into the future can involve significant uncertainty, but decision makers, in particular, expect analysts to look beyond the current situation. You may want to posit multiple outcomes, especially if your confidence level is low.[4]

---
[4] Methods for generating multiple future outcomes are described in Heuer and Pherson, *Structured Analytic Techniques for Intelligence Analysis*, Chapter 6: Scenarios and Indicators, p. 119.

Regardless of how confident you are, almost every *outlook* section should identify the most important variables or drivers in determining the outcome. The key word that every outcome discussion should contain is "if." As a business or intelligence analyst, your job is not to "predict" using a crystal ball, but to explain possibilities using your knowledge and expertise. *Outlook* discussions can be made more useful by explaining what indicators you will be watching for as potential signals that a certain outlook will come to pass. *Outlook* sections can come in a variety of forms:

- A single outlook tied to an unspecified time frame: When you have high confidence but are unable to project a specific time frame. The development will occur when certain conditions are met.

- Multiple outlooks tied to an unspecified time frame: When significant uncertainty is present and you are unable to project a specific time frame. Multiple paths are possible when certain conditions are met.

- Multiple outlooks for one set timeframe: When significant uncertainty exists even in the short term, you may want to hypothesize alternative outcomes linked to various variables and provide indicators.

- Multiple outlooks for different time horizons: When high uncertainty exists in both the short term and long term.

Multiple outlooks are more helpful when you can indicate which outcomes are more likely to occur and the reasons why.

What are the implications of the development for your target audience?

The *implications* discussion should focus on how the issue in question directly affects your target audience, whether that is a policymaker, law enforcement official, or a business executive; and what opportunities and options might achieve a desired result or avoid an undesirable outcome. The more specifically you identify a target audience, the more precisely the *implications* section will provide value added to that decision maker.[5]

The *implications* section should be cast from the perspective of how the main actor in your paper would respond to various initiatives rather than how your target audience should behave to achieve a certain result. Every decision involves some degree of uncertainty and an upside or downside risk. The analyst's primary task is to lay out that uncertainty and risk rather than to simply posit a particular course of action. Capturing uncertainty in judgments is much more difficult when they are cast from the perspective of "you need to consider this." Moreover, the target audience may be aware of information unavailable to the analyst. The target audience—and not the author of the analytic study—is usually the decision maker and your paper should reflect this important distinction.

Discussion of the consequences of an issue for a country's neighbors or a company's business competitors is part of the *outlook*—not *implications*—discussion. This distinction between the implications for other countries

---

[5] See the Customer Checklist, Getting Started Checklist, and Issue Redefinition techniques in Heuer and Pherson, *Structured Analytic Techniques for Intelligence Analysis*, Chapter 4: Decomposition and Visualization, p. 45.

and companies and your target audience is important because it helps you to retain sight of the main purpose of the paper: advancing the interests of your target audience. Below is an example of a paper that would address all five focal questions.

Addressing the five focal questions:

Improved Public Perceptions of the United States in Freedonia Likely To Drive New Policy Initiatives

What: Improved US image and popularity in Freedonia.

Why now: Factors driving the change in the perception of the United States.

Impact so far: Overtures/signals from Freedonia suggesting interest in closer ties.

Outlook: What are the prospects for improved relations with the United States?

Implications: *How improved relations could benefit US interests and objectives.*

As noted in the previous chapter, you may not need to address all five analytic questions in every paper. In some cases, you may have just two. Use the following questions to help determine which you should address and which you can ignore or give only cursory attention:

What is the event or development that is driving your paper? The most critical decision you will make—and the one into which you will have to put a lot of thought—is where to begin your paper. This initial focus is the first part of the paper's bottom line: what your readers need to know that they do not already know; the second part is what it means for your readers' interests and goals. If you are not clear about where you want to begin your paper, the likelihood of a muddled organization increases dramatically. Typically what results is a paper that meanders and is **circular** rather than a paper that begins with a clearly defined focus and marches forward.

Once you have made the decision where to begin your paper, the subsequent sections answer follow-up questions that support your key analytic takeaway. An element of the original question should be stated or implied in these follow-up questions. If that element is missing, the paper may stray off course. In the example on page 16, a paper could begin with **no change in policies** despite an improved US image, followed by a section that explained why **no change in policies**, and then a discussion of what the United States could do to bring about **a change in policies** that is more favorable to the United States. In this paper, you would have a *"what?"*, a *"why now?"*, and an *implications* section. As you can tell by comparing this organizational scheme with the scheme in the initial example, the two papers are much different despite sharing a common focus. Where you begin your paper makes a huge difference.

The implications section should be cast from the perspective of how the main actor in your paper would respond to various initiatives rather than how your target audience should behave to achieve a certain result.

What are the interests and needs of your target audience? Are readers interested in a broad range of issues related to a development, or in a smaller, more focused aspect of the problem? What time frame is of particular interest to them given the level of their likely engagement with the issue over time? If you want your target audience to go beyond the title and read your paper, you have to focus on its interests.

> **Focusing on the target audience:**
>
> **Target audience:** World Bank Officials
>
> **What:** Freedonia seeking to increase population five-fold by 2050.
>
> **Possible focus of a "*why* now?" section:** What do the population goals indicate about the leadership's current mindset?
>
> **Possible focus of an *outlook* section:** Assessment of obstacles and likelihood of reaching population targets.
>
> **Implications:** *Given the uncertainty associated with this assessment and your audience's lack of interest in developments so far out, the analysis in this section should be skipped.*

How knowledgeable of the issue is your target audience? The sooner you provide value-added information, the more likely your target audience is to continue reading. If readers are already familiar with an event and no new developments update the story, discussing the event in detail could bore them. They may stop reading your paper because they believe it is unlikely to tell them anything that they do not already know. A paper in this case might begin with the "*why now?*" or an *outlook* section.

Anticipate your audience's substantive questions (see Figure 5). Think consciously about what your reader will know about an issue. You may discover avenues of research and discussion for your paper that you had not considered before. For example, if you are writing about a company's efforts to market a widget that is not selling and your assessment is that the company is likely to continue to do so (based on an uptick in advertising for the widget and statements from company officials), the question many readers will ask is why? If you are writing about a country's apparently clumsy efforts to influence an election in another country, some readers may wonder whether the country is also engaging in more nuanced, sophisticated efforts to sway voters.

What information do you have? This is a simple, but important question. For the "*why now?*" and *impact so far* sections, you may have very little information, especially if your paper is focused on a recent development. Recent developments may not have had enough time for any *impact* at all to have emerged. You probably will have little choice but to provide some reasoned speculation on future impact in an *outlook* section. If many possible variables could be influencing an actor's motivation, a discussion of "*why now?*" probably works better in a text box rather than in the main body of the paper. Your uncertainty regarding motivation could also be captured with caveats and conditional possibilities in an *outlook* section that includes a reference to the text box.

Figure 5. Key Questions for Organizing Your Research and Analysis

1. **Identify** the key issue or problem with which your principal customer is currently wrestling or likely to confront in the near future. Remember that customers at different levels are likely to be dealing with different "levels" of decisions on the issue.

2. **Brainstorm** a list of focused key questions relating to the topic that the customer is likely to ask or that the customer anticipates someone will ask her. Answering a focused question that consumers are currently asking increases the chances your product will be useful. It will have immediate appeal. Answering a set of focused questions is easier than structuring a detailed outline from scratch.

3. **Add** any questions to the list that the customer may not be asking but probably should be. Draw on your expertise and analytic tools to add any questions that the customer—because of their more limited time and knowledge of the topic—has not yet thought about.

4. **Select** the questions on the list that you can answer or provide a useful perspective. If you cannot answer an essential question, consider starting work to get the answer. If you have received a direct question from a customer, be sure to include it near the top of your list.

5. **Prioritize and organize** the list of questions to guide your collection, collaboration, and research—and the outline of the finished product. Your organized set of questions now becomes a roadmap to begin researching and drafting the finished product. Remember that the questions may change as your research and drafting proceed.

Significant confusion among some sections can arise because the *"why now?"*, *impact so far,* and *outlook* discussions can easily overlap. These focal questions are part of a continuum that relates to the actor's motivations and goals over time.

The *"why now?"*, *impact so far,* and *outlook* sections are in reality a mix of what your readers need to know and why it is important to them. Some call this the *"so what of the so what?"* when it focuses on what actions the reader should consider doing next. A discussion of an actor's motivation for taking a certain decision, for example, focuses on the actor, but that discussion also could be useful to your target audience in deterring or encouraging that decision. Similarly, an *outlook* section that discusses future developments is of direct interest to your target audience if those developments affect actors, such as another country or a related business, in which your target audience has an interest.

Be careful to maintain consistency between the focus of each section and the focus of its paragraphs' topic sentences. *"Why now?"* and *impact so far* sections look back, while *outlook* sections look forward.

- If developments that have occurred in response to the *"what?"* are harbingers of future developments and are cited as part of the basis for the *outlook* judgments, the paper does not need a separate discussion of *impact so far*.

- Similarly, the *"why now?"* and *outlook* sections can merge into one section. Discussion of what the actor hopes to accomplish can be combined with a discussion of what is likely to be accomplished, provided a common thread can be identified. If Freedonia acquired new technology to build a new weapon system, the *"why now?"* and *outlook* questions are part of the same discussion. If, however, Freedonia acquired new technology for producing a weapons system out of concern about Bleakistan's intentions, the *"why now?"* and *outlook* questions are much different discussions.

- If you use *"why now?"* and *impact so far* information to support judgments in an *outlook* section, you can reference past developments in the topic sentences if they serve as a lead to an outlook-like judgment. For example: The economic gains achieved by currency devaluation are likely to prompt another devaluation.

On page 20 are examples of possible organizational schemes for various hypothetical papers. The examples are intended to demonstrate how papers could flow organizationally from one section to the next.

Organizing your paper:

R&D Spending Straining Pharmaceutical Company A's Cash Flow Position

Target audience: Business executives at an investment company
What: How much Company A is spending.
Why now: Seeking to develop breakthrough medicines.
Impact so far: Forced to take on significant debt.
Outlook: Stock price likely to continue to fall.
Implications: Purchases of Company A stock risky but large upside given depressed stock value.

Equipment Acquisition Major Coup for Timbuktu's Chemical Weapons (CW) Program

Target audience: Government officials and analysts
What: What is this equipment (how it helps) and how did Timbuktu acquire it?
Why now: Probably would not address the question of why they acquired the equipment unless something is specifically driving the acquisition.
Impact so far: None so far (it just acquired the equipment).
Outlook: Discussion of timeline for producing CW agents and factors that might accelerate or slow that timeline.
Implications: What can the United States do to delay or prevent that timeline if anything?

John Doe Heavy Favorite to Win Presidential Election in Freedonia

Target audience: Government officials and analysts
What: Nothing.
Why now: Nothing.
Impact so far: Nothing.
Outlook: Basis and caveats for judgment that John Doe is going to win by a landslide.
Implications: What is John Doe seeking from neighboring states?

Expansion of State Police's Role in Border Control Forcing Cutbacks in Other Missions

Target audience: Governor's aides and staff
What: State police now devoting 20 percent of officers and resources to border control.
Why now: Nothing, aides and staff well aware of federal law passed last year.
Impact so far: Reduced commitment of officers and resources to highway patrols.
Outlook: Increased speeding and more highway fatalities likely.
Implications: None, intended primarily to inform.

New Legislation in Bleakistan Unlikely to Slow Drug Trafficking

Target audience: Government officials and analysts
What: If the focus of the paper is on the assessed inability of the legislation to stem drug trafficking, details and background information on the legislation might work best in a text box or weaved into the first few sentences of the opening paragraph, especially if the target audience knows that the legislation passed and its history.
Why now: If nothing is relevant to your target audience about the motivation for the legislation, an explanation focusing on why now also could be addressed in text box above.
Impact so far: None, legislation just passed.
Outlook: Discussion of factors that are likely to limit the effectiveness of the legislation on drug trafficking.
Implications: What can the government do to mitigate these factors?

4. Prepare a Detailed Outline

The first step in planning an outline for your paper is to craft a working title. A working title will help you clarify the focus of your paper and create a conceptual framework for organizing it. Make sure the title names the key actor or trend and uses an active verb to introduce the *"so what?"*. If you cannot condense your message into a pithy, engaging title, then you lack the clear message that is essential for a successful and informative analytic piece. Do not settle for descriptive titles that note what the paper is about.

Making titles analytic:

A title that lacks an analytic message:

Assessing the Political Strengths and Weaknesses of President John Doe

An alternative title with an analytic message:

President John Doe Struggling to Assert Power

At this point, you also should be able to write a lead sentence or working summary. The title and lead sentence tell the story in a nutshell. A working summary can come in a variety of forms depending on how extensive the analysis: one sentence for a short paper and a set of bullets or even multiple paragraphs for longer papers. The lead sentence or summary highlights new insights, warnings, changes, and critical implications. It conveys the key takeaway(s) for the consumer. If you are having difficulty writing this lead sentence or summary, you need to do more analysis. Once you have completed the paper, you must go back to the title, lead sentence, and working summary and refine them.

As we noted in Chapter One, the most important requirement for a well-organized paper is a precise mission statement that captures the analytic bottom line. The more precise the mission statement, the easier the paper will be to organize because the path to get to that key judgment is more direct. A well-organized paper by definition takes the shortest possible path between where the paper begins and the key takeaways or analytic judgments the reader has harvested by the time they finish reading the paper.

The more vague and ambiguous the mission statement, the broader the path to those judgments and the easier it will be to go off on a tangent or include material that is only peripherally relevant. If you think of your analytic bottom line as an argument or a story, then the organization of the paper merely retraces the steps to that conclusion or outcome.

A detailed outline is exactly that: an outline with details. You cannot prepare a useful outline without details, and you cannot thoroughly understand an issue and generate insightful analytic judgments without a solid grasp of the information. At this stage in the process, a thorough assimilation of the material and the preparation of a detailed outline should occur simultaneously. Preparing a detailed outline is part of the writing phase, but it is also part of the thinking phase. The more detailed the outline, the better the odds are for insightful and accurate analysis. The objective is to have the analysis fit the facts, not the facts fit the analysis. If you do not start with the facts, you may end up trying to make the facts fit the analysis.

The objective for a detailed outline is to create a roadmap for writing your paper down to the paragraph level. By preparing an outline or sketching your line of argument with a flow diagram, you will have generated ideas that will serve as topic sentences. The next step is to assemble a body of supporting information to support those topic sentences. Analysts who are good writers and thinkers can pull together a coherent paper without a detailed outline, but this is asking for trouble. They can leave material out, miss important analytic points, and ignore key gaps in logic. It is better to create and follow an outline **one step at a time**.

If you are having difficulty preparing a detailed outline down to the paragraph level, three explanations are possible:

- You have not given adequate attention to your target audience's interests, and your effort to prepare a detailed outline is undertaken in a vacuum rather than focused on key questions the target audience is likely to have.
- You have not immersed yourself enough in the information. You may have lots of ideas to build paragraphs around but not a lot of details for each paragraph.
- You have a solid grasp of the information but have not spent enough time and energy assimilating this material as part of a coherent story. All the facts are there, but you have not developed a coherent line of argument or the organization is confusing, repetitive, or lacks clear flow.

The objective for a detailed outline is to create a roadmap for writing your paper down to the paragraph level.

As you review your research, consider adopting the following system for organizing your paper—or develop a system of your own! Make note of the information that is relevant to the subject and file each piece of information (not the report) in a separate folder or file (hard copy or soft) according to whether the information relates to what has happened, why it has happened, what impact it has had, where it might go, and what it may mean for your target audience. You may be taking multiple bits of information from one report and filing the data in separate folders and files.

Within each folder, look for patterns, sequences, similarities, and differences in the information that will help you to build separate analytic judgments and, therefore, separate paragraphs. Structured analytic tools as well as maps, charts, and timelines are useful in extracting significance from the data.

For each data point, attach a generic descriptor to help you connect it to other data points. For example, if the 212th Brigade of the 69th Rifle Division was ordered to deploy to the front, a simple descriptor such as "troop deployments" would work. Research background information on the data point to help you understand its significance. Is the 212th Brigade important? When has it deployed before? To the same area or to a different location?

An excellent analytic tool for creating a detailed outline is a wiki page where collaborating analysts can input the data that they are discovering as well as develop the analysis. A wiki page allows everyone working on a project access to the same material. Ideas can be generated and refined as the data is collected, staving off the hardening of individual analytic mindsets leading to debates rather than discussions. Analysts can input various interpretations of the data to accompany specific bits of information as well as suggest areas of additional research. A wiki page enables everyone involved in an analytic project to be instantaneously "on the same page."[6]

Analytic writing works most effectively if it organizes the analyst's thinking and information in a logical way, highlighting the most important concepts, ideas, and judgments for the reader. It follows conventions common to journalism—by emphasizing the need to put the bottom line up front—but differs from academic writing in which the logical flow presents the researcher's evidence in increasing order of significance and builds to a conclusion. In analytic writing, the title and lead sentence convey the core message, key judgments are often showcased in bold print, and the most important part of almost every assessment comes at the end in the outlook and implications sections (see Figure 6).[7]

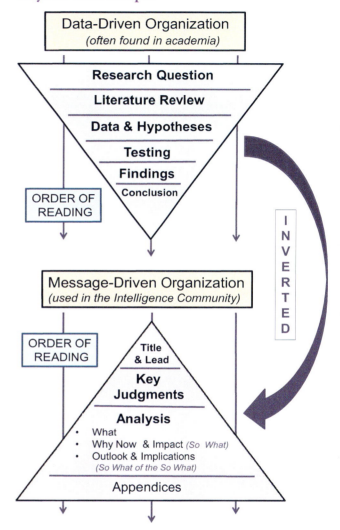

Figure 6. The Inverted Triangle: Contrasting the Ways to Write a Paper

Community, placing the most important things (specifically, the topic sentence or key message of the paper) at the top of an upside down pyramid. Others, however, have found the image confusing, arguing that the supporting evidence should form the base of the pyramid as it provides the foundation for the analysis or the rationale for the topic sentence. Our solution to this conundrum is to use a triangle to mirror how a paper is organized, reflecting the amount of space each section takes up and then illustrating how this order can be inverted, contrasting a data-driven organization of a paper with a message-driven approach.

---

[6] The use of wikis to draft collaborative papers is discussed more fully in Heuer and Pherson, *Structured Analytic Techniques for Intelligence Analysis*, Chapter 12: A Practitioners Guide to Collaboration, p. 293.

[7] This figure is offered as a possible replacement for the Inverted Pyramid model used by many in the Intelligence

Figure 7. How to Generate a Detailed Outline

Working title: Britain: Massachusetts Rejecting Political Dialogue With Crown

Target audience: The King of France

The What: Unhappiness with Crown Growing

Paragraph main point: The new leaders of the opposition parties in Massachusetts are opposed to heavy British taxation and judge that most residents of Massachusetts share this view.
- Statements by various leaders and citizens regarding their views on taxation and how they have evolved.
- How high is taxation?

Paragraph main point: They also believe they are getting little back in the way of services and protection for their taxes.
- Concern about the poor status of the harbor in Boston and the need for renovation. When was the harbor last improved? What has been the effect of having a run-down harbor?
- Weak response of British government to Indian massacre of colonists in western Massachusetts last month in which 14 were killed and 12 kidnapped. How did the British respond to previous massacres?

The Impact: Splits Emerging Among Colonists

Paragraph main point: Splinter group has broken off from Independence Now Party (INP).
- Group formed a new party, the We-Love-England party, on 25 May.
- Party is made up mostly of merchants worried about losing business.
- Nathan Makeabuck's editorial about impact of political tension on exports to England.

Paragraph main point: Concern growing among INP members that England will try to exploit differences among colonists.
- Sam Adams' warning that Crown will do this. Who is Sam Adams? Is he important?
- John Adams' plea for unity among colonists. Who is John Adams?
- Is there any evidence Crown planning to do this?

Outlook: Resolving Differences Unlikely, Revolution Possible

Paragraph main point: Political differences between George V's government and Massachusetts colonists have become irreconcilable as the English dismiss the opposition parties in Massachusetts as irrelevant and the colonists harden their position.
- Prime Minister Gladstone accused the opposition parties of inciting unrest and drinking coffee instead of tea, the ultimate insult. What is the negotiating style and persona of Gladstone? Is he a known bluffer?
- Britain's War Minister called John Adams a "raving lunatic." How have the British referred to John Adams before?
- Sam Adams in a press conference reiterated demand that colonists pay less tax and get more services. He also said the colonial government was composed of nothing but British lackeys and called the governor a "complete toad." What kind of backing among the colonists does Sam Adams have? Does his opinion matter?

Paragraph main point: Prospects for change in British position are not good.
- British officials are portraying a solution to the crisis in glowing terms, but the colonists have rejected the reforms as insignificant.
- An editorial by the London Times praised the steps taken by George V to resolve the crisis as a "great deal" for the colonists.
- The officially-controlled British press is ignoring the crisis, covering more mundane issues like the opening of a new castle.

Paragraph main point: If Britain maintains hardline position, political crisis will grow and probably prompt colonists to take drastic action against the British.
- Polls show colonists not in favor of backing down. What is the reliability of polling data? What is the trend in sentiment based on polls?
- George V burned in effigy last week. Has this ever happened before?
- Brainstorm issue of what drastic action the colonists could take.

Preparing an outline should be an iterative process. An initial outline should include a core point for each paragraph that is captured in a topic sentence and a short description of the supporting information. As you begin writing, ask yourself: what additional questions do I need to research? Are the paragraphs in the right order? Does some of the information fit better in another paragraph? Is material in a later paragraph redundant with material in an earlier paragraph (see Figure 7)? As you write, new information will come in and new insights will occur, prompting additional research, new judgments, and adjustments to the outline. A final review by you and the reviewers will lead to additional changes in the paper's flow. This cycle does not end until the paper is published.

A well-organized paper is "efficient" in the sense that the reader's time is not wasted: the flow of the paper moves step-by-step in a forward direction to the outlook or implications for the target audience. A well-written paper does not spin wheels in any section with a lot of irrelevant material or repeat relevant information already covered. A reader who reads only the topic sentences in a well-organized paper will be able to glean the main analytic points without having to read the entire paper.

Indicators that your tentative detailed outline probably needs revision include:

- The topic sentence is a statement of fact; no analytic conclusion can be found. As a result, the flow of the analytic storyline is broken as you read from one paragraph to another.

- The topic sentence is not directly relevant to the paper's mission statement. Either the paragraph needs to be deleted or the topic sentence revised.

- A paragraph includes multiple analytic judgments. If the analytic focus of a paragraph is ambiguous, the storyline will appear disjointed to the reader.

Assuming each paragraph is analytic, relevant, and focused on one central analytic point, the organization may still need revision because:

- Important judgments related to the flow of the analytic argument are missing.

- The analytic storyline does not consistently move forward but meanders or moves backward. Indicators of a possible problem with analytic progression include the same supporting information appearing in multiple paragraphs or the topic sentence being out of sync with the analytic section ("*what?*", "*why now?*", *impact so far, outlook,* and *implications*) in which the paragraph is located.

- The sequence of paragraphs could be better arranged within an analytic section by taking into account the relative importance of each paragraph and shared issues among some paragraphs that suggest their juxtaposition is in order.

Review your outline looking for gaps or discontinuities in the analytic progression of the storyline. Paragraphs are missing or need to be moved when:

- Analytic leaps occur between paragraphs. For example, an analytic judgment that a country's president is likely to be ousted in a coup if he raises taxes needs to be supported by proof that the president wants to increase taxes.

- Successive paragraphs do not advance the story either because the main judgment in the second paragraph is essentially the same or it is misplaced. If, for example, you have a judgment in one paragraph that a country's harsh rhetoric to influence an election in another country will continue because the first country judges the strategy is working, and in the next paragraph you have a judgment that the rhetoric has become harsher in recent weeks, the storyline has moved backward. The topic sentence in the second paragraph is not well crafted for an *outlook* section, which by definition is looking forward. That topic sentence instead is more appropriately written for a paragraph in a "*what?*" section.

Detecting paragraphs where the analytic line is essentially the same requires a close read. In many cases, the paragraphs can be combined.

- Paragraph 1 Topic sentence: Freedonia has made significant efforts to expand its financial sector in Bleakistan but has achieved only modest success [defined later in the bullet points as establishing only five banks doing limited business].

- Paragraph 2 Topic sentence: None of the banks have major investments in Bleakistan, where their focus is on motorboat loans and checking accounts. *(These paragraphs can be easily combined.)*

How should I order my paragraphs?

If you have multiple developments, drivers, or points to discuss within one analytic section, you should determine the optimum order in which to present this material. Are there similarities or common threads in the paragraphs that suggest they should be juxtaposed rather than

separated by another paragraph or paragraphs? Are some developments more important than others? Is there a timeline that is important to convey?

In some cases, a logical order exists. In what order would you present a discussion of: a) who will vote for candidate X?; b) who will vote for candidate Y?; and c) how many voters are leaning toward candidate X? Typically, maintaining the consistency of any continuum offers the best approach for ordering related information.

Putting things in logical order:

What are some options for organizing a three-paragraph *"what?"* section discussing various indications baseball slugger Luis Caisera, who currently plays for the LA Dodgers, wants to play in New York?

- Luis' positive comments about living in New York and playing for the Yankees.

- Recent trips of Luis' agent to New York.

- **Luis' comments suggesting he wants to play for another team** besides the Dodgers.

This last fact probably should be moved up to be in the first paragraph in the "what?" section. It sets the stage for Luis wanting to play in New York and would keep paragraphs based on Luis' comments juxtaposed.

Strive for balance in the progression of the analytic storyline that reflects the relative priority of the analytic judgments in your paper. For example, if you have identified three factors that are likely to drive sales of a widget through the roof, and one of them is a much more important driver in your estimation, begin with that driver and allow for more discussion of it over the other two. Just because information is available does not require you to use it. Your target audience will consider a long-winded discussion on an issue that is less important than others in the paper a waste of their time.

Part III: Writing the First Draft

A successful analytic paper is one in which the target audience understands, accepts, and remembers the paper's bottom line as well as the underlying analysis that supports it. This requires well-constructed topic sentences that help readers track the paper's analytic progression. The key to getting the analysis accepted is to provide the readers all the information they need to understand the basis for the supporting judgments.

Getting the reader to remember the ideas in your paper requires direct and straightforward language. Your presentation should facilitate the assimilation of your argument or storyline by the reader. The draft should minimize extraneous material that might obscure or confuse the conclusions you want to emphasize.

Crafting an effective analytic paper and getting it right depends on you, the author. Your paper will only be read once by the intended reader. Do not expect to get a second chance to clarify, explain, or elaborate on what you have written. In Part III, we discuss how to:

Build Paragraphs Around Good Topic Sentences
Answer All Likely Questions
Order the Supporting Information
Treat Peripheral Information Separately

5. Build Paragraphs Around Good Topic Sentences

Tightly focused paragraphs are the building blocks of effective analytic papers. The key to crafting a tightly focused paragraph is a good topic sentence. They are the portal that draws you into the paragraph. Like the paper's bottom line, you should be able to articulate each paragraph's main point without hesitation. A long-winded explanation of the paragraph's main point is an indicator of a paragraph that does not have a main point or has too many.

By definition, an analytic topic sentence has some level of uncertainty associated with it, meaning that the author may not have 100 percent confidence that the judgment is correct. Analytic topic sentences often include caveats based on the author's confidence in the judgment, such as "almost certainly" or "probably;" verbs, such as "suggest" or "indicate," that imply a judgment or conclusion; or conditional phrases that begin with "if" or "provided."[8]

> *The most important requirement for a good topic sentence in an analytic paper is that it includes analysis, i.e., a judgment or conclusion that helps the reader track the line of argument in the paper.*

Think of the paragraph's topic sentence as the *reason* for the paragraph; ask yourself why you are writing the paragraph. The topic sentence expresses the paragraph's purpose, the main idea that you are trying to convey to the reader.

If the topic sentence lacks an analytic judgment:

- Readers do not know what to think and have to analyze the supporting information and come to their own conclusions, provided they have the patience to read the remainder of the paragraph. They may reach a different conclusion about the significance of the information in the paragraph than the one you intended. At this point, you are no longer the analyst but just a researcher collating information for the reader.

For the author, as well as the reader, the importance of good topic sentences is almost impossible to overstate. Delete the topic sentence, and that paragraph will become an immediate challenge for the reader, even if the remainder of the paragraph is focused and well-written. The most important requirement for a good topic sentence in an analytic paper is that it includes analysis, i.e., a judgment or conclusion that helps the reader track the line of argument in the paper.

---

[8] The best way to deal with levels of confidence in analytic judgements is reviewed in Pherson and Pherson, *Critical Thinking for Strategic Intelligence,* Chapter 17: How Should I Portray Probability and Levels of Confidence?, p. 185.

- The paragraph has no focus and can drift in all sorts of unrelated directions. Without a purpose for the paragraph, everything is fair game for inclusion—a recipe for a long, meandering discourse. In a paragraph without an analytic topic sentence, one idea can easily lead to a related idea and so on until what is being discussed at the end of the paragraph bears no relation to the issue that was addressed at the beginning. A lot of material should be cut, but no basis exists to evaluate what to cut and what to keep.

- Decisions on what the next paragraph should be about are made in a vacuum, and prospects for a well-organized paper diminish rapidly. The analysis in the topic sentence is what provides the continuity and connection between the paragraphs that compose the overall analytic story. It is the glue that holds the paper together. If a paragraph lacks an analytic judgment, the analytic thread needed to move the paper to the next paragraph will be missing. You can always go back to the previous paragraph and develop the analysis in that paragraph's topic sentence, but such an approach still leaves an analytic dead end in the middle of your paper. If any paragraph does not serve an analytic purpose, you should delete or break it up, and distribute the information to other paragraphs where the material supports an analytic point.

Analytic topic sentences serve as a guide that helps readers work their way through a paper. In an analytic paper's early sections, the discussion often focuses on judgments in which there is more certainty; for example, revealing what has already occurred or pronouncements that have already been made. These initial paragraphs probably will do little more than summarize what has already transpired. The significant analysis that you are providing is your judgment that these developments are important and deserve to be brought to the reader's attention. More complex judgments that typically occur later in your paper—perhaps in the *outlook* or *implications* section—contain more uncertainty. In this instance, the topic sentence should include both the judgment as well as a short synopsis of the rationale for the judgment.

Some of the most common functional types of topic sentences are:

- **Summarization:** Typically a laundry list. Example: The government last week cut taxes, lowered interest rates, increased spending on infrastructure, announced a new budget, and appointed a new Treasury Minister to slow the economic downturn.

- **Generalization:** An overarching characterization or assessment of individual items as belonging to a certain group or a certain type. Example: Most of the steps the government has taken to improve the economy involve efforts to boost consumer spending.

- **Comparison:** An assessment of similarities and differences or how things have changed (what is new?)—in most cases a comparison of some aspect of the present with the past. Example: The reliability of the regime's security forces is more problematic now than it was six months ago, given growing support in the military for the opposition.

- **Causation:** An identification of the causes of past or ongoing events. Example: The anti-matter weapons program is proceeding slowly because of equipment shortages, poor quality control, and a lack of technical expertise.

- **Evaluation:** An assessment of the significance of one or more recent developments that explains their significance in a broader, future context. Example: The acquisition of the new bows and longer range arrows almost certainly has given the Huns military superiority over the Goths, whose bows and arrows are notoriously inaccurate and have less range.

- **Future assessment:** An assessment involving a likely future outcome or impact. Example: The Huns are likely to use their newly acquired military superiority to reacquire territory they conceded in an earlier conflict with the Goths, especially if the leader of the Huns dies and is replaced by his son, who is much more aggressive than his father.

Well-written topic sentences, in addition to being analytic, are:

- **Precise:** Uses exact language to convey a well-defined, specific analytic judgment.
- **Clear**: Uses straightforward and direct language that allows the reader to quickly understand the analytic judgment.
- **Accurate:** Summarizes or captures correctly the essence of the supporting information; the analytic judgment and supporting information are in sync.
- **Consistent:** Addresses the same issue in the same way as the supporting information.

- **Complete:** Covers all the main analytic issues discussed in the remainder of the paragraph.
- **Digestible:** Enables the reader to assimilate the main analytic points without having to take notes or draw a flow chart.

Analytic paragraphs typically have one topic sentence and a block of supporting information. These two components are interdependently **linked**: the supporting information drives what goes in the topic sentence, and the topic sentence determines what belongs in the supporting information block. A well-crafted topic sentence and the supporting information block should mesh like the cogs in two precisely machined gears. The topic sentence captures the main idea in the paragraph, and the supporting information persuades the reader to accept this main idea as valid.

Be Precise

Precision and clarity are not interchangeable concepts. Precision relates to the lack of ambiguity in the topic sentence's main idea; clarity is the extent to which that idea is understandable as written. The reader does not receive a precise analytic judgment when the topic sentence only hints at what the paragraph is about. Topic sentences that lack precision could just as well begin with the sentence: "This paragraph is about _____." Take the reader all the way, not half way, to your idea. Below are examples of topic sentences that only hint at what the paragraph is about, they are crystal clear but not at all precise.

- The conduct of various Roman generals in Gaul varied, depending on whether they had served and fought in Africa earlier in their career. A more precise topic sentence: Roman generals in Gaul who earlier in their careers served and fought in Africa were more brutal and took fewer prisoners than commanders who did not serve there.

- Dwight Eisenhower played a pivotal role in the victory of the Allied Powers in WWII. As opposed to: Dwight Eisenhower's skill in managing difficult subordinate commanders from different countries minimized the amount of infighting among Allied generals and kept their attention focused on defeating Germany.

The analysis in the topic sentence is what provides the continuity and connection between the paragraphs that compose the overall analytic story.

The common denominator in the two examples above and the main culprit in many imprecise topic sentences is ambiguity that leaves the reader asking, **"What is the paragraph's central point?"** A precise topic sentence is open to only one interpretation. In the last example above, Eisenhower could have played a pivotal role as the lead military commander for the Allies in a number of ways. With an imprecise topic sentence, readers have to read the remainder of the paragraph to see if it contains information of value. With a precise topic sentence, readers understand the paragraph's central point even if they do not read anything else in the paragraph. They may not be convinced if the supporting information is lacking, but at least they know where you stand.

The topic sentences in the examples above may be good placeholders in your first or second draft, but after rereading the entire paragraph a few times, a more precise topic sentence should emerge. This is not just a writing issue but a thinking issue as well. As you become more familiar with the information driving the topic sentence, the precision of your analysis should increase. Do not get hung up on writing the perfect topic sentence in the first or second draft. Write and revisit. Each time you read the topic sentence's supporting information, you are processing that information. The reality of writing analytic papers is that you are thinking and assimilating information before, while, and after you write.

Making the topic sentence more precise:

Topic Sentence: The ruling party is reluctant to condemn the terrorist group because of the threat that the terrorist group might pose to the party.

It is important to establish the nature of the threat. Is the party concerned that the terrorist group would attack party officials or party offices if it condemns the attack? Or is the party concerned that citizens sympathetic to the terrorists might not support the party if it condemned the attack?

Scrubbing your topic sentence for precision means taking little for granted regarding your reader's knowledge of the issue. In some cases, adding precision to your topic sentence may require inserting only a word or two. That may not seem like much, but it can make a major difference to a reader who is not as familiar with the information as you are.

Improving precision by providing more content:

What one or two critical words are missing in the following two topic sentences?

Several key legislators are maintaining that allowing **deductions for** housing expenses, health insurance, and education fees would reduce taxes for the poor.

What kind of deductions? Are these deductions going to be created or expanded?

The government hopes that **recent charges** brought against journalists and TV newscasters of **alleged criminal offenses** such as indecent exposure, drug possession, and reckless driving will make it easier for the government to intimidate and control domestic media outlets.

Are these criminal offenses real crimes or trumped up charges?

Be Clear

The reader does not receive a straightforward and direct analytic judgment when you use language that is more convoluted than it needs to be; when there are internal inconsistencies in the language; when you use "passive voice" sentence constructions; or when the topic sentences emphasize secondary, background material.

- **Convoluted language:**
  - The government is seeking to define its own ascendance as a break with the past eight years of left-leaning governments and as the demise of regulation and government economic interference.

- **Internal inconsistencies:**
  - The societal and political changes brought on by the collapse of the government have ~~witnessed~~ **spurred** the emergence of radical groups. *(Changes are not people; they cannot witness an event.)*

  - After 48 UN sanction votes condemning his rule, Gen. Diehard in May ~~surrendered~~ **succumbed** to international pressure and resigned. *(Most of the time one country surrenders to another country.)*

  - The divisions will report to the commander**s** of the Northern and Western military district, **Gen. Diehard and Gen. Shootstraight, respectively.** *(Unless Gen. Diehard has an alter ego personality named Gen. Shootstraight, commander needs to be changed to commanders.)*

- **Reliance on context:**
  - The risk of gang violence in the county **may increase** following the acquittal of gang leader John Doe. *(The impact of the acquittal is implied.)*

- **Passive voice:**
  - **Security will be improved by** the new identity verification system. *(Active voice: The new identity verification system **will improve security**.)*

- **Undue emphasis on background information:**

  o Freedonia **is deploying peacekeepers to Dictoria but** may also send them to Bleakistan out of concern that the spate of violence there last year will lead to renewed, all-out fighting between insurgents and tribal entities. *(If this is not a main idea, it belongs in a dependent clause: Freedonia,* **which is deploying** *peacekeepers to Dictoria,* **may also***…)*

Find the Right Words. Look for the most direct and straightforward way to state the paragraph's main analytic point. If you cannot articulate the paragraph's bottom line without having to read the text to get it "right," your language is too convoluted. Parroting the main analytic message as it is worded in the example below might be difficult unless you have memorized it. A good rule of thumb is to use words your target audience will quickly recognize rather than words that might force the reader to consult a dictionary.

Avoiding tongue twisters:

The phrase: The spike in intra-tribal violence following the election is a reflection of the growing weakness of the tribal-controlled political system to maintain stability.

A better sentence would be:

The spike in intra-tribal violence following the election suggests that the potential for political instability is growing.

To eliminate internal inconsistencies and inappropriate word choices, mentally delete peripheral details in the sentence and focus on the main point of the sentence, usually the subject and verb and the first few words after the verb. Be on the look-out for internal consistencies particularly when you are reviewing sentences that have compound verbs. The verb needs to be consistent with the subject in the first part of the sentence.

Eschewing internal inconsistencies:

The phrase: The **legislature** probably **will ratify** the amendment and **return** to their home districts.

Need to rewrite to say:

The **legislature** probably **will ratify** the amendment and **its members will return** to their home districts.

If you string too many modifiers together in front of a subject of a sentence or clause, the reader may have to reread the complete reference to get a clear sense of what the subject is. Try not to use more than two modifiers even if it is grammatically correct. Instead, use phrases and other clauses that allow the readers to catch their mental breath.

Using modifiers properly:

The phrase: *"Bleakistan's five-year timber production and export goals…"*

Should be rewritten to state:

"Bleakistan's five-year goals for timber production and exports…"

Use Active Voice. If you are attributing cause and effect, try to make the subject of the sentence the cause, and the verb and the direct object the effect. This will eliminate many passive voice constructions and make your sentences more direct. In passive constructions, the reader often has to make assumptions regarding your central point based on context. In active constructions, the reader has much less room for doubt. A verb's "voice" or its relationship to the nouns in the sentence is "active" when the actor or subject performs the action. This is usually a clearer, more concise, and interesting sentence structure. A "passive" sentence structure means that the actor is absent or is the object of the action specified by the verb.

Passive voice can be confusing if the reader needs to guess who the actor is. It forces the writer to add words that are weak, including non-specific pronouns, such as "there" or "it," the preposition "by," or compound verbs. In addition to being more direct, active voice constructions are often shorter and more concise than passive voice constructions.

Using active voice:

Incorrect Passive Voice Formulation: The state police obtained the warrant, and the suspected terrorist was arrested. *(Did the state police apprehend the terrorist or did someone else?)*

Correct Active Voice Formulation: The state police obtained the warrant and arrested the suspected terrorist.

Passive voice is grammatically correct, but discouraged in analytic writing. You can use it when you intentionally want to hide the actor or emphasize the idea over the actor. This is often the case in scientific or technical writing, but also explains why technical documents often sound bureaucratic and boring. In short, use passive voice consciously and sparingly if you cannot find an acceptable active alternative.

Focus on the Main Idea. Topic sentences that emphasize background or secondary material can take the focus off the main analytic judgment and cause confusion in the reader's mind as to the paragraph's main point. Minimize background noise; place secondary, background information in adjective clauses; and use the primary subject/verb construction to highlight the main analytic judgment.

Avoiding topic sentences with misdirected focus:

Topic Sentence: Paul Jones worked early in his career for the Wheeling and Lake Erie Railroad and later became a seminal figure in the history of the NFL.

If this paragraph is about his football career, a better topic sentence would be:

Paul Jones became a seminal figure in the history of the NFL after working early in his career for the Wheeling and Lake Erie Railroad.

Do not use the first sentence to establish context and the second sentence to make the main point. Make the main point first and then establish context if you cannot do this in a single sentence.

Making the main point first:

The actions of John Doe, founder of Top Foods, a NASDAQ-listed caterer, and the majority owner of the football team New York Whales, has caused a media sensation among sports journalists. **Doe announced his intention to buy the Plymouth Rockers, one of the longstanding bitter rivals of the Whales.**

The information in the second sentence should be the focus of the first sentence.

Put your topic sentence's main point as close to the start of the sentence as possible. If you begin with a long dependent clause, the focus of the sentence can become that clause. Beginning a topic sentence with a short dependent clause is unlikely to be a problem.

Eliminating long dependent clauses:

Incorrect: After amassing 2 million men, 5,000 tanks, 10,000 artillery pieces, and 20,000 trucks on the border, Hitler invaded the Soviet Union in June.

Correct: Hitler invaded the Soviet Union in June after amassing 2 million men, 5,000 tanks, 10,000 artillery pieces, and 20,000 trucks on the border.

With topic sentences that lack clarity, the reader can in time decipher what the analytic judgment is without reading further into the paragraph. With topic sentences that lack precision, the reader gets an idea but has difficulty going beyond that general idea to a specific, well defined judgment without reading further into the paragraph. In both cases, the reader has to slow down and work harder. With convoluted topic sentences, the reader assumes the role of writer and, with imprecise topic sentences, the role of thinker or analyst.

Be Accurate

Analytic judgments in the topic sentence should accurately reflect the supporting information—and vice versa. After reading your paragraph, the reader should be able to see how you got from the supporting information block to the analytic judgment in the topic sentence. Topic sentences are not properly written, however, when the topic sentence says one thing and the supporting information says or appears to say something different. At that point, you must either revise the topic sentence or supply additional supporting information to provide a basis for accepting the analytic judgment in the topic sentence.

Be Consistent

A skeptical target audience will be looking for inconsistencies that weaken or undermine your analytic judgments. Also be on guard for analytic leaps that go beyond the supporting information. Inconsistencies can creep into a topic sentence in several ways:

- The analytic judgment that is supported in the paragraph extends to a related but different judgment that is not supported.

- The activities noted in the supporting information are mischaracterized in the topic sentence. For example, criticism of an institution for wasteful spending becomes criticism of an institution for being corrupt.

- The actors noted in the supporting information are mischaracterized in the topic sentence because assumptions were made that were not warranted. For example, individual lower-level officials involved in illegal arms sales become "the government" involved in illegal arms sales despite the absence of evidence indicating that the actions of the lower-level officials were sanctioned.

- The supporting information is overstated or understated in the topic sentence in terms of its extent, duration, consistency, or likelihood. For example, isolated events are given broader significance than warranted.

Be Complete

A complete topic sentence serves as an umbrella for the main points in the paragraph. Think of the topic sentence as a **roof on a house**, and the walls and vertical beams as the supporting information holding up the roof. Are all the main actors noted in the supporting information represented in the topic sentence either specifically or as part of a group? Are all the main events, developments, explanations, outcomes, or implications represented? Do you need to expand your topic sentence to cover all the main ideas in the paragraph, or move some ideas to other paragraphs?

Ensuring the topic sentence is complete:
The news media in Freedonia are calling for stricter enforcement of municipal safety ordinances for private nursing homes after a fire last week destroyed one home and killed 40 senior citizens. This was the sixth fire this month at a nursing home in which residents were killed.
• The Townsville Times questioned how these nursing homes were able to obtain licenses and government approvals while a television report speculated that the owners of the nursing homes acquired the approval through bribes.
• The Daily Planet noted that such fires are likely to continue unless the government steps up enforcement and levies large fines on those homes that are not in compliance with the safety regulations.
• The Weekly Tribune, which also called for stricter enforcement of government regulations, **urged the government to dedicate more resources to building safe public nursing homes** so that senior citizens do not rely on private homes, which are considered "death traps."
The main idea in the third bullet needs to be reflected in the topic sentence.

Topic sentences also can fail the completeness test if obvious ancillary analytic questions related to the main judgment are not explained. These questions are often follow-up "why" and "how" questions that can be answered in a short phrase. Be alert to these possible questions.

Addressing the "why" and "how" in a topic sentence:
Initial formulation: Protests have trailed off over the past several weeks, probably as a result of opposition from community leaders.
Why are they opposed?
Better formulation: Protests have trailed off over the past several weeks, probably as a result of opposition from community leaders, who believe **that protests would be counter-productive**.
How would they be counter-productive?
Best and most informative: Protests have trailed off over the past several weeks, probably as a result of opposition from community leaders, who believe **that protests would be counter-productive in forcing the regime to make political concessions**.

Be Digestible

The reader must be able to readily assimilate the main idea in a topic sentence. Long topic sentences may be unavoidable, but shorter and simpler sentences are better when possible.

- A topic sentence can overwhelm the reader when it includes too much background information that is not essential to understanding the main idea. In this case, some of this material, which is often in auxiliary clauses, can be moved to other sentences in the paragraph.

- Topic sentences can confound a reader when they include too many related ideas that the reader is unable to process quickly. In this case, breaking the paragraph up and creating a second paragraph is advisable.

- No single formula for crafting a good topic sentence is without flaws. Topic sentences can include multiple actors, main events, new developments, explanations, outcomes, or implications—provided they maintain enough precision in language to remain meaningful to the reader. Another requirement is that the supporting information for the analytic judgment can be included in the paragraph without creating enormous "word bricks."

Writing valid topic sentences different ways:

- John Doe's frequent visits to Iowa over the past six months suggest he either intends to run for president or is considering moving there after his Senate term expires next year.

- John Doe's recent visits to Iowa over the past six months and numerous media interviews in which he has cast himself as committed to solving America's problems suggest he intends to run for president.

- John Doe's numerous media interviews, frequent public appearances around the country, and recent visits to Iowa over the past six months suggest he intends to run for president or is positioning himself as a viable vice presidential candidate.

How many aspects a main idea in a topic sentence will have is determined by the paragraph's role in the overall scheme of your paper, the length of the paper, and how much information you present. For example, if you are writing a paper on how pop music in America during the 1960s and 1970s influenced the views of young Americans on government, race relations, and premarital sex, you probably have at least one separate paragraph devoted to each issue, with each paragraph's topic sentence focusing on pop music's impact in just one area. If, however, you are writing a broader paper—but not a necessarily longer paper—on all the forces that have helped change the views of young Americans on race relations and sex, and pop music was one of many factors, you might have one paragraph on pop music and its impact on all of these issues.

Craft a Solid Second Sentence

The second sentence in a paragraph can serve a variety of roles. In some cases, the second sentence provides context that helps the reader understand the main idea rather than proceeding immediately to providing examples and argumentation that directly attests to the validity of the main idea in the topic sentence. This context can come in different forms, including historical or technical information.

Using second sentences to provide context:

Roman generals in Gaul, who earlier in their careers had served and fought in Africa, were more brutal and took fewer prisoners than commanders who did not serve there. **Battles between Rome and Carthage were known for their ferocity and large numbers of casualties that sometimes numbered in the thousands.**

- Bullet citing specific behavior of forgiving Roman generals.
- Bullet citing specific behavior of unforgiving Roman generals.

The second sentence also may elaborate on the main point in the topic sentence, providing additional details and specifics, or extend the analysis by linking the main idea in the first sentence with other new ideas. In these cases, the supporting information in the bullets often supports the second sentence more than the first, and the second sentence should be considered part of the topic sentence. Two topic sentences should be used if the alternative is a long, cumbersome, and confusing single topic sentence.

Sometimes the second sentence takes a much sharper analytic turn to a much different judgment. This second analytic sentence, which should be considered part of the topic sentence, typically occurs in paragraphs where the main focus of the paper switches from one actor or judgment to another. In some cases this occurs because new, alternative judgments are being posited. Such sentences often are found at or near the end of the paper. As a general rule, you should limit the number of alternative judgments in a paragraph to one.

Creating a bridging sentence that elaborates on the topic sentence:

John Doe is likely to face challenges to his party leadership given dissatisfaction with the state of the economy, numerous personal scandals involving sexual harassment, and his abrasive personal style. **Several party officials, including Mark Doe, Jane Doe, and Paul Doe, have made public statements suggesting they want to be the party's next leader and are more qualified and able than John Doe.**

- Bullets on the political ambition and strengths of Mark, Jane, and Paul Doe.

Creating a bridging sentence that extends the main idea of the topic sentence:

A stationary El Niño off South America is responsible for the increased frequency of heavy snow in northern Virginia during the past several winters as well as drought-like conditions during the summer. **This weather pattern has contributed to an increase in road rage incidents during the winter, the imposition of water-use restrictions during the summer, and more children going to their neighborhood pools.**

- Bullets on road rage, water restrictions, and pool use.

6. Answer All Likely Questions

For readers to understand and accept your analysis, the paper needs to give them all the information they need when they need it. Otherwise they will resort to guessing or making assumptions on their own, asking themselves, for example: "Why is that?", "How so?", "What does that refer to?", "What am I to make of that?", or "How is that different?". You may know exactly what you are referring to in your paper or how to explain the apparent inconsistency, but the reader cannot read your mind. Eliminate these **barriers** to effective writing.

You can lose readers or make them work harder than necessary in at least three ways:

1. Inconsistencies, omissions, or disconnects in the line of analysis, or between the key judgments and the evidence, lead the reader to wonder what to think or what to believe.

2. The author makes unwarranted assumptions about the reader's level of knowledge and familiarity with the subject matter, i.e., the reader knows less than the author thinks he knows.

3. The reader is confused by different likelihood assessments related to the same judgment, ambiguous references, mischaracterization of previously introduced factual material, invalid comparisons, data that do not add up, or missing transitions between sentences, ideas, and paragraphs.

Be Explicit and Make Linkages Clear

One of the ways an analytic judgment is left unstated in a topic sentence is to follow a factual statement with two or more related factual statements and assume the reader will understand the significance of the first factual statement by assimilating the information that follows.

> **Ensuring proper connections in a paragraph:**
>
> **Poor example with connection implied:** The town government waited a week before discounting the rumor of an impending eruption at a nearby volcano. One year ago, the town government denied a rumor about the growing likelihood of an eruption but three days later the volcano erupted, and local officials were blamed for the large loss of life.
>
> **Good example with connection made explicit:** The town government waited a week before discounting the rumor of an impending eruption at a nearby volcano probably to avoid criticism if the volcano erupted and people were killed. One year ago, the town government denied a rumor about the growing likelihood of an eruption, but officials were blamed for the large loss of life when the volcano erupted three days later.

The analytic relevance of the supporting information to the paragraph's main point must be readily apparent to the reader, or it will appear to be a distraction. The whole purpose for including the supporting information—to make the paragraph's analytic judgment credible to the reader—is undermined. When reviewing supporting information in a paragraph, routinely look for the link between the supporting information and the analytic judgment. If you know the answer, but it is not in the paper, you need to **build stronger links** in the paragraph. Look for ideas in the topic sentence that are not addressed in the supporting information. In some cases, your reader may be able to make some reasonable guesses, but in other cases, the reader may be completely lost.

> **Making sure you provide complete information:**
>
> Paul Revere's actions over the past week suggest he has been chosen by the American rebels in Boston to warn of any pending British troop movement. Revere has been seen repeatedly practicing a hand signal involving a lantern that denotes whether the British troops are moving by land or sea, according to a British loyalist. In addition, **Derek Jones, a close friend and known collaborator of Revere**, has been looking to buy the fastest horse he can find, according to another British loyalist.

> **Building stronger links in a paragraph:**
>
> After two years of slow growth, growth in the industrial sector is poised to top 6 percent this year. Most of the companies in this sector are now employee-owned.
>
> *The connection between the uptick in growth in the industrial sector and most companies being employee-owned needs to be established.*
>
> **Did you mean this:** Most of the companies in this sector are now employee-owned, creating a highly motivated work force that is achieving record increases in productivity.
>
> **Or this:** Most of the companies in this sector are now employee-owned, creating a highly motivated work force willing to work overtime to meet customer orders.

Similarly, if a relationship or connection is present between proper nouns in your topic sentence and proper nouns in your supporting information, make that linkage explicit. Every time you make the reader "read between the lines," you slow him down or cause confusion.

Use transitions to smooth the argument's flow. Transitional words and phrases help orient the reader to your line of reasoning. They link ideas, paragraphs, or other parts of speech, and preview what is coming next. You should consciously look to use them in key locations in your product. Transitions can emphasize a point ("the most compelling evidence"), compare or contrast ("similarly," "as opposed to"), clarify or add information ("for example," "additionally"), enumerate ("next," "last"), or summarize ("as a result," "in conclusion").

Include Explanatory Information

Analytic papers are not mystery novels. Do not keep your readers in suspense. If new information is introduced and important explanatory or background information is left out, you can lose your reader. Some befuddled readers may pause, and go on a fishing expedition if they assume they have missed the explanatory material. Their search for an answer may involve small details not critical to your main point like **different colored rocks on a pathway**. This can quickly divert them from the main focus of your paper.

When you make specific references, consider if you have caused the reader to ask a question. For example, if your paragraph focuses on the assessment of how well the president of one country works with another, and readers are unaware that the two presidents ever met, the importance of one president's assessment of the other may take a back seat to finding out when the two met. Often this explanatory material comes much later in the paper, prompting the reader to go looking for it.

- You almost always need more explanation when you are characterizing an event as a significant numerical follow-up to previous events, such as the president's third major press conference on foreign relations. *(During what time frame? When were the first two given?)* Or the president's third major address. *(What was the subject of the first two?)*

Answering questions before they arise:

If you can be specific with little or no increase in the number of words, it will answer potential questions before they arise.

Initial sentence: "The Western-educated prime minister who is known for her personal style in dress…"

Better formulation: "The Harvard-educated prime minister who is known for wearing a hijab…"

The best place for inserting material that identifies individuals or explains unique or ambiguous terms is the sentence in which the person or term is first introduced. If the explanation is too cumbersome for insertion as a clause in the first sentence, place it in the following sentence.

- This applies to technical terms—such as depleted uranium—as well as foreign-language concepts—such as *velyat-e-faqih*—or coined phrases—such as "axis of evil." Many readers may be familiar with the term "axis of evil" but perhaps not all. How many readers would know that *velyat-e-faqih* refers to a system of governance in which an Islamic jurist is given the right to govern until the appearance of the 12th Imam? One tip-off that a term needs explanation is that you are tempted to put it into quotation marks or to italicize it. Defining your terms immediately keeps everyone on the same page.

- Explanation is required when the information is not explicit or is confusing because of translation issues, a problem that can occur when citing information from foreign media.

    o The CEO said that problems with setting up the production line—*a reference to an ongoing strike at the facility over alleged safety issues*—will set back production at least six months.

    o The prime minister said that some political groups have not "realized the nature" of the committee, *a reference to the different views some groups have on the committee's mandate and its responsibilities.*

- Identify potentially unfamiliar individuals and proper nouns, including named events—such as the Boxer Rebellion—sooner rather than later. The introduction of someone by name is not helpful if the reader is not familiar with that person. John Doe could arbitrarily be changed to Mr. X and the significance of the name may not amount to much. The question "Who is this?" would still pop into the reader's mind.

The best place for inserting material that identifies individuals or explains unique or ambiguous terms is the sentence in which the person or term is first introduced.

- Organizations and their acronyms need explanation the first time they are introduced in the text. Typically, the explanation involves the organization's area of responsibility. More importantly, it may also involve its relevance to the analytic point being made. After you spell out the acronym, use of the acronym later in the paper is acceptable unless your paper is filled with too many acronyms to remember. In general, try to keep the number of acronyms to a minimum, especially those with which your reader may not be familiar. The more often an acronym is cited in a paper, the less likely a reader will be to lose track of what the acronym represents. Readers are more likely to lose track of acronyms that are cited only a few times and play a secondary role in the story. In this case, use a few words to identify the entity or process rather than rely on the acronym.

Some information requires additional explanation to be meaningful to your target audience; without context, the reader cannot gauge the significance of the information. This is particularly true when discussing numerical data of almost any kind, but it also applies to other types of information, such as sourcing descriptions.

Providing context for numerical data:

- Energy exports last year amounted to **$2 billion dollars** in large part because several large oil fields began production.

How much of an increase from the previous year was this? The number by itself tells the reader little.

- High school teachers in Freedonia routinely shorten lessons in public schools to allow more time to tutor and earn additional income after school. Salaries for public school teachers in Freedonia average around **1,000,000 pesos per year**.

What is the average salary in Freedonia? What if it is 10,000,000 pesos? How much are they underpaid?

Eliminate Potential Sources of Confusion

Make sure the probability statements you attach to similar judgments are consistent throughout the paper. Analytic judgments consist of two components: the substance of the judgment and the associated likelihood. Analytic judgments that are similar in substance but different in assessed likelihood are two different judgments. Analysts can disagree about the exact meaning of "almost certainly," "probably," "likely," "might," and "could," but almost everyone would agree that they perceive a difference between "almost certainly" and "probably" or between "likely" and "might." Also be attuned to possible *likelihood creeps* in your judgments.[9]

---

[9] An extensive discussion of the proper use of probabilistic language appears in Pherson and Pherson, *Critical Thinking for Strategic Intelligence*, Chapter 17: How Should I Portray Probability and Levels of Confidence?, p. 185.

Analytic judgments need to be consistent and to support one another. A judgment that the leader of Bleakistan is likely to resign because of domestic pressure is not consistent with the judgments that the leader of Bleakistan would never back down in a crisis and is probably under pressure from his wife to remain president. Similarly, the evidence cited to support an analytic judgment needs to be consistent within the paragraphs, or the reader will become confused about the message. If there are analytic inconsistencies, you need to explain them. They will become unnecessary **bumps in the road**, making it harder for the reader to follow your line of analysis. If you cannot explain them, some modification of the analytic judgment is in order.

> **Explaining an analytic inconsistency:**
>
> Spanish King Ferdinand is likely to invade Austria in response to the Austrian Emperor's decision to hang Ferdinand's nephew. Ferdinand has a long history of attacking countries that mistreat his relatives.
>
> - In 1631, Ferdinand repeatedly attacked the British Fleet after the British King threw his mother in prison.
> - In 1625, Ferdinand invaded Prussia after Prussia rounded up all his cousins and shot them in a public square.
> - In 1622, the Spanish King did nothing when Russia sent his brother to a prison camp in Siberia. **Ferdinand reportedly wanted to retaliate against Russia but was persuaded against the idea because of the enormous distance between Spain and Russia.**
>
> *The last sentence is needed to account for the inconsistency.*

Confusion also can arise when you use a generic description that could refer to any one of a group of similar subjects introduced previously. Similarly, it may not be clear if you introduce a new noun later in the paragraph using a generic description and relationship that is not clear to previously introduced subjects. In both cases, a more specific and less generic reference is preferable unless the focus of the paragraph and the location of the sentence make it absolutely clear.

> **Avoiding confusion with multiple subjects:**
>
> Another case of food poisoning was reported during the past week, suggesting ineffective government monitoring of the restaurant industry. John and Jane Doe became ill while eating in a restaurant and were admitted to the hospital. At least five other cases have been confirmed this month. The Great Spaghetti Restaurant has agreed to pay $20,000 to the **victims.**
>
> *Does this refer to John and Jane Doe or to the victims in the other cases? If it refers to the Does, you need additional language or you need to move it so it follows the sentence on the Does.*

Confusion can arise in the reader's mind when a paragraph contains multiple subjects and references back to these subjects are open to misinterpretation. Make sure pronouns refer to the right actor. A pronoun works well if it is used after a sentence in which you identify the actor, unless more than one actor is referenced in the preceding sentence; then you need to identify the actor by name.

Make sure that the reference is clear when using the modifier "other." Problems can arise when you have more than two potential references that fit the description of "other." For example, let's assume your paper is discussing non-Salafist and Salafist groups in Bleakistan, and you have segregated the Salafist groups into two types: the die-hard Salafists and the middle-of-the-road Salafists. The following paragraph could cause confusion: "The die-hard Salafists and the middle-of-the-road Salafists are opposed to any delay in the implementation of Sharia law in Bleakistan. The die-hard Salafists also are opposed to cooperation with the Muslim Brotherhood, but the other groups are not." Does "other" in this case refer just to the middle-of-the-road Salafists or to the non-Salafist groups as well?

Avoid reliance on ambiguous modifiers and generalizations in your supporting information block that can mean different things to different people. "A large, angry crowd" could be 50 people on a street corner shouting slogans or several hundred people throwing Molotov cocktails at security personnel.

Confusion can arise in the reader's mind when you are contrasting information and the difference is not clear. Readers may reread the sentence, assuming they missed something, but the difference is not there, often because you are comparing "apples" and "oranges." You can compare the temperament of dogs with the temperament of cats, but a comparison of the size of dogs with the temperament of cats is not a comparison. If you use language such as "but" or "however" that suggests a comparison, the reader will look for one. Keep comparisons focused on comparable things.

Avoiding confusion with ambiguous terms:

Topic sentence: Protests erupted across the country within hours of the prime minister's announcement of the new austerity measures.

By "protests" were we referring to:

In the capital of Freedonia, a crowd of several hundred people set tires on fire and overturned cars in the business district. The large, angry crowd continued to grow through the evening hours.

Or does the following sentence describe the "protests?"

In Freedonia's second largest city, some 5,000 people marched in unison singing the country's national anthem. The massive-but-peaceful demonstration ended in the early evening hours.

Discussion of numerical data in your paper must be clear and "add up," otherwise the reader experiences *numbers gridlock.* Data that are not clear and consistent immediately confuse and frustrate readers, particularly if they are unable to sort the data out quickly.

Keeping comparisons comparable:

Poor sentence: Only one person was killed in the protests, but the **violence included attacks** against government buildings, businesses, and private residences.

The number of casualties is being compared with what was attacked, and the reader has to read between the lines.

Better sentence: Only one person was killed in the protests, but the violence was **nonetheless extensive and** included attacks against government buildings, businesses, and private residences.

A more valid comparison with number of casualties.

Poor sentence: The country's minority population is subject to severe economic discrimination and harsh workplace mistreatment. Its petitions, **however,** appear designed to parallel the petitions of the majority who want a more representative political system.

What is being contrasted with this "however" is not clear.

Better sentence: The country's minority population is subject to severe economic discrimination and harsh workplace mistreatment. Its petitions, however, **downplay the importance of** economic demands and appear designed to parallel the petitions of the majority who want a more representative political system.

In this construction, it is clear that the author intends to contrast the views of the minority with the majority.

A common problem when presenting data that appears inconsistent is that "apples" and "oranges" are being compared, but this fact is not explicit. Fixing this problem typically requires adding language to resolve the inconsistency. If you are comparing "apples" with "apples" and the data are inconsistent, acknowledge the inconsistency so the reader does not stop reading and pause to figure out the inconsistency. A simple sentence prefacing the data is all the reader needs. For example: Estimates on the number of widgets sold last year vary widely. Another problem that causes confusion is when the data in the text are not consistent with their presentation in the graphics (see Figure 8).

Figure 8. Making Life Easier for the Reader: Consider Graphics Early and Often

Incorporating graphics into an assessment or report helps analysts make a compelling case by conveying information more vividly. Graphics or visuals serve two main functions:

- **Summarizing data** so that the reader can more easily absorb it.
- **Showing relationships** that add meaning to the data.

You can convey large amounts of data extremely efficiently in a well-designed graphic or video. For example, visual displays using a bar graph or line chart enable readers to immediately comprehend trends or patterns. Senior officials and managers can use—and often rely on—graphics to understand underlying dynamics, make accurate comparisons, and draw conclusions in a matter of seconds. Often a cartoon or a photograph can convey a message far more effectively than a paragraph of text.

For a more detailed discussion of how graphics can support your analysis, see Pherson and Pherson, Critical Thinking for Strategic Intelligence, Chapter 18: How Can Graphics Support My Analysis?, p. 197.

Do not forget to include dates. Dates provides important context necessary to understanding the importance and significance of events and statements. The crossing of a border before a declaration of war is a much different event from one that occurs after war has been declared. Dates are easy to work into the text, and leaving them out can cause unnecessary confusion. Include the date when the event occurred or the statement was made, not the date of the report. The reader can obtain the latter information from the endnote.

Making your numbers add up:

Poor formulation: The academy lacked sufficient space to reach its goal of training 1,000 new dog catchers. Media sources report that during January-August only 900 dog catchers graduated from the academy.

Better: The academy lacked sufficient space to reach its goal of training 1,000 new dog catchers every six months. Media sources report that during January-August the academy graduated only 900 dog catchers.

Unless you know for certain when someone will read or publish the paper, avoid date descriptions such as yesterday, last week, or recently. Some readers in your target audience may read your paper after its publication, and they will have to calculate what "recently" means, thereby slowing them down.

How much of the date to include depends on how recent the event or statement is relative to the timing of the paper or report. As a general guideline, if the event occurred within the past several weeks and within the same calendar year, include the day and month. If the event occurred several months ago, but within the same calendar year, the month probably is adequate unless the specific date carries significance. If the event occurred within the past 12 months, but in the previous calendar year, use the reference "last November" or "last June."

> **Including dates correctly:**
>
> **Topic Sentence:** Winston Churchill's understanding of economics was limited, leading him to make a number of decisions that brought economic hardship upon Great Britain, especially the poor.
>
> *Not a bad hypothetical topic sentence except for one small but critical omission noted in the last sentence of the next paragraph.*
>
> He oversaw Britain's return to the gold standard which resulted in deflation and high employment, a decision he regarded as one of his greatest mistakes. Moreover, Churchill's budget measures were roundly criticized as befitting the prosperous and detrimental to the less fortunate. **Churchill pursued these policies while he was Chancellor of the Exchequer from 4 June 1924 to 8 August 1926.**
>
> *Day and month are probably not necessary in this example. You can easily insert the information in this last sentence into the paragraph's first sentence as a phrase.*

If the event occurred more than a year ago, month and year probably are adequate unless the specific date has some significance. If you want to add more precision, inserting "early," "mid," or "late" in front of the month will do it. For events that occurred several years ago or longer, the year probably is enough information for your reader. Again, you can be more precise about timing by inserting "early," "mid," or "late" in front of the year.

If your description of the sequence of events is not clear, the reader will pause and try to figure it out. You can describe a sequence of events either looking forward or backward, but do not mix or interchange the sequence. Try to keep them consistent with one another relative to the order in which they occurred.

> **Describing sequences of events correctly:**
>
> **Incorrect:** The suspect admitted that he stabbed a young woman to death **after striking her with his car when she tried to record his license plate number.**
>
> **Correct:** The suspect stabbed the woman when she **tried to record his license plate number after he hit her with his car.**

Use quotes sparingly. They can be particularly effective in conveying a word or phrase whose meaning or context would be lost in paraphrasing. For example, a foreign official publicly calling a neighboring country's president a "buffoon" communicates much more than saying that the foreign official has strong doubts about the intelligence of the neighboring country's president. The use of the term "buffoon" suggests the foreign official has little respect for the neighboring country's president and feels strongly about it.

Avoid long quotes bookended by quotation marks; paraphrase this material instead or work key elements of the quote into a sentence that is easier to read but captures the full flavor of what was said. Long quotes can be a distraction to the reader. In cases where you are citing a non-English speaker, a complete literal translation can cause more confusion than clarification, especially when the syntax of the statements and the words themselves do not readily translate into easily digestible English.

> **Using long quotes effectively:**
>
> **Literal translation:** Marc Anthony asked Caesar: "What is the use of long spears? Are not our short swords adequate to defeat the German hordes?" Anthony said Caesar replied that "He only wanted to teach the barbarians a lesson they will not forget. If the Army only has short swords, the victory will not be overwhelming."
>
> **Improved citation:** Marc Anthony claimed that Caesar wanted the Army to have long spears in order to achieve an "overwhelming victory" and "teach the barbarians a lesson they will not forget."

7. Order the Supporting Information

When arranging supporting information within paragraphs, the author has several decisions to make, including: how many bullet points, the order of the bullet points, the order of information within bullet points, when to break up bullet points, and when to delete some of the information.

Each paragraph contains a new analytic judgment, a separate but important piece of the overall bottom line. Supporting information comprises the **building blocks** that form the foundation for the anlytic judgments in your topic sentences. Optimizing the order of supporting information in individual paragraphs makes it easier for the reader to understand, accept, and remember that judgment, which in turn helps the reader to understand, accept, and remember the paper's bottom line.

The Number and Order of Bullet Points

The optimum number of bullet points in an analytic paragraph is between two and four. Two will do the job most of the time. Remember, the objective of the information in the bullet points is to support the main point in the paragraph, not to demonstrate that you are a thorough researcher. Keep the bullet points that best serve this function and delete the rest.

If you have a large number of bullet points, examine the information in the bullets to see whether you can combine some without creating a word brick. You may need to delete some less critical information in your bullets or make a major effort to be more concise. Another alternative is to compare the information in the bullets to see whether the similarities and differences among them are evidence of two analytic points, not just one. In this case, separate the information into two paragraphs.

Think of each bullet point as a stand-alone, discrete example that supports the main idea in the topic sentence. Do not use two bullets that taken together only equate to one example of supporting information. Having a lot of details in a bullet that more directly relate to a previous bullet rather than the main idea in the topic sentence takes the emphasis off the paragraph's main idea. The information in the two bullets needs to be combined into a single bullet. If it turns out to be a very long bullet, you need to cut some text. An alternative to deleting the text is to move this background material into a text box. Let the main idea in your topic sentence be the litmus test for what gets cut or moved.

Think of each bullet point as a stand-alone, discrete example that supports the main idea in the topic sentence.

> ### Combining information to improve flow:
>
> From 1950 to 1955, economic growth in Europe varied considerably by country with some countries posting strong growth.
>
> - The economy in France has soared over the past five years, averaging almost 7 percent per year, while growth in Italy has also been strong, averaging well over 5 percent per year.
> - France's economy has benefitted from the soaring price of wine, strong growth in the airline industry, and new home construction, while the election of a new Pope, Louis I, who is widely popular among many Catholics in other countries, has boosted tourism in Italy.
>
> *The information related to France should be combined into one bullet and the same done with regard to the information on Italy.*

The two-degrees-of-separation rule—a good general guideline—is to have no more than one sentence per bullet that provides additional context for the information that directly supports the topic sentence. To avoid longer bullet points that appear to take on a life of their own separate from the main point in the topic sentence, place the additional contextual material in a text box.

> ### Deleting unnecessary contextual material:
>
> During 1950-55 economic growth in Italy, which averaged 7 percent per year, outpaced all other European countries. Increased tourism and offshore oil production in Venice spurred growth in Italy. The election of a new Pope in 1953, Louis I, who was widely popular among many Catholics in other countries, was the primary driver that boosted tourism. **Louis I was popular among other Catholics because of his efforts to reform the church and his love of baseball.**
>
> *Delete the last sentence; the bullet is becoming more about Louis I than Italy's economy.*

Supporting information can be arranged in a number of ways:

- Order of importance to your argument.
- Chronological order, with the most recent information first.
- Chronological order, with the most recent information last.
- Order of detail, with the more general information first.
- Similarity, grouping like information together.
- Logical order in which the bullets represent a chain of reasoning that proceeds to a conclusion.

The order that you select depends on the paragraph's objective: are you trying primarily to persuade, show a trend, describe a situation at different levels of detail, contrast different data points, or outline an argument? In the example below, what is the underlying purpose of the paragraph below, and what does it imply for the order of supporting information in the bullet points?

> ### Putting bullets in chronological order:
>
> During the past several months, the National Socialist German Workers' Party (NDSP) terror group **has begun** to attack Germany's right wing parties—especially the Germany First (GF) party—and the German police, signaling a major shift in the terror group's view of its former political allies. The NSDP previously had targeted only left wing politicians and government officials.
>
> *The paragraph's primary purpose is to show a change has occurred and to mark when that change began.*
>
> - An NSDP hit-list discovered by the Bavarian police in **May 1932** included the right wing General Heitel and the police chiefs for every major German city.
> - **In January 1932** the NSDP assassinated several GF leaders and bombed a GF office in Munich.
> - **In April 1932,** the NSDP carried out a suicide attack at a GF rally, killing more than 20 people.
>
> *Start with the second bullet because it marks the first event. The last bullet would become the second bullet in order to maintain chronological order.*

Parallel Structures and Like Items

Maintaining a parallel structure between the topic sentence and the supporting information minimizes the amount of mental whipsaw that the reader has to endure and allows the reader to more easily process the information. This applies to individuals, countries, or concepts in the topic sentence as well as to any comparison that is being made: the pro and con sides of an argument, the advantages and disadvantages of a development, or the potential rewards and risks of various policy options. Discuss one, then the other, and then move on to a new paragraph.

Organizing supporting information group by group:

Topic sentence: Britain and France finally are prepared to declare war on Germany if Hitler invades Poland.

Provide information on Britain, then information on France.

Topic sentence: The British and French decision to sign a defense treaty with Poland, may force Hitler to forgo an invasion of Poland, but the risk is high that Hitler judges it is a bluff.

Continue with a discussion of factors that might lead Hitler to back down followed by a discussion of factors that might lead him to go ahead with an invasion.

When organizing information within a paragraph, group like pieces of information together, otherwise your paragraph will appear choppy. The same key word appearing in two separate sentences typically is a tip-off that this information is related and probably should be juxtaposed in the paragraph. Pull this information together to improve the paragraph's flow.

Similarly, when presenting a list of items within a sentence, it is helpful to keep like items next to each other. Doing so helps the reader compartmentalize and remember the information.

Keeping like items together:

Poor construction of bullets: To get into the US Naval Academy, I will need to:

- **Take several AP courses, participate in several extracurricular activities, and have a very high GPA.**
- **Demonstrate leadership potential outside of the classroom, and score well on the SAT.**

Of the items in the list above, separating academic and non-academic issues allows the reader to assimilate one generic issue before moving on to another.

Better construction of bullets: To get into the US Naval Academy, I will need to:

- **Take several AP courses, have a very high GPA, and score well on the SAT.**
- **Participate in several extracurricular activities and demonstrate leadership potential outside of the classroom.**

Strength of Supporting Information Versus Timeliness

When each item of information supports your topic sentence more or less equally, you probably want to begin with the most recent information first. If you are making an analytic judgment about a current situation, and you can cite supporting information from last week, it makes your analysis appear up-to-date and worth reading.

If, however, your supporting information varies considerably in strength of support for your paragraph's main point, the best approach is to begin with your strongest supporting information first, even if it is not your most recent evidence. That said, the information must be recent enough to still be relevant. Beginning with your strongest evidence buys you credibility and keeps the reader interested and engaged, provided it is not too dated.

The remainder of your supporting information should be arranged according to the extent it supports your paragraph's main point. Insert the dates for this supporting information toward the middle of your sentences rather than at the beginning so the focus is on the evidence and not on the dates.

When each item of information supports your topic sentence more or less equally, you probably want to begin with the most recent information first.

If the information that provides the most direct support for your paragraph's main point is your oldest information and the rest of your supporting information is an order of magnitude weaker, you probably should begin with the oldest and strongest information. In this case, you can note in your topic sentence that the more recent information is much less conclusive. If you begin with your best, but apparently dated, evidence, and do not acknowledge this up front, the reader may conclude you lack objectivity and are promoting an agenda.

Information in a Series or a Progression

If your objective is to show a sequence of events culminating in an outcome, particular pattern, or trend over time, then the optimal order of your bullet points would be chronological, placing the most recent information last.

- Language in the analytic topic sentence for a paragraph intended to show a culmination might include "a series of steps leading to" or "setting the stage" for some major event, historical discontinuity, or technical breakthrough.

- Language in the topic sentence for a paragraph intended to show a trend typically involves a set of comparisons—life in Freedonia is getting progressively easier, or arms purchases by Bleakistan have steadily decreased since 2005.

In paragraphs where you are seeking to show a trend or a series of steps that lead to an outcome, place the time element at or near the beginning of the sentence or bullet point. That will help to reinforce your judgment about a progression of events or trend in the data. To break up the repetition of "on such and such a date," use intermittently the time interval between events.

> **Placing the time element up front to show a trend:**
>
> - In March 1938, Germany annexed Austria with little objection from Britain and France. The Austrians welcomed German troops with open arms.
>
> - Five months later, Britain and France conceded Czechoslovakia's Sudetenland to Germany in exchange for a pledge from Berlin that Germany would have no more territorial demands.
>
> - In March 1939, Germany occupied the remainder of Czechoslovakia, prompting Britain and France to promise to defend Poland.
>
> - In September, after German forces invaded Poland across a wide front, Britain and France declared war on Germany.

General Versus Specific Information

If you have a mix of general and specific information—especially if the specific information concerns exceptions to the general information—most readers are receptive to having the general information first, especially if it provides them with "buckets" that allow them to group and store the specific information.

- For example, information that the Non-Aligned Movement (NAM) voted unanimously to defeat a UN resolution should come before information citing the reasons that key NAM country 1 and key NAM country 2 cited as their rationale for voting against the resolution.

- If, however, your focus is on key NAM country 1 and key NAM country 2, you want to begin with those countries first and then put their action into context or compare their vote with the vote of other countries.

Similarly, with various sample sizes of numerical information, it is best to begin with the large samples and work toward the smaller.

> **Ordering bullets from large sample sizes toward smaller samples:**
>
> - Half of all Third World countries have a sizable share of their population living in poverty.
>
> - This share rises to about 75 percent for Third World countries in Africa and to almost 100 percent for Africa's sub-Saharan countries.

Bullet Points that Compare

If you are making comparisons between past and present and the comparison can be made in a sentence that is not too long, provide the data point or idea for the past first—perhaps in a dependent clause—and let the data point for the present be the subject of the sentence. This construction makes the current information the main focus of the sentence and provides the necessary context for the reader to compare and understand the data point or idea for the present at the most opportune time for the reader: before you move on to another sentence. It also makes for a shorter sentence. If it is too complicated for one sentence and one bullet point, discuss the present data point or idea first and then the past data point or idea in a separate bullet point, but use some transitional language—such as "however" or "in contrast"—to lead into the second data point or idea.

Using bullets to compare past and present:	**Constructing bullets on the same subject:**

Using bullets to compare past and present:

Good construction: My commute to work is now one hour each way. Two years ago when I lived in Winchester, my commute was two hours each way.

Better construction: My commute, which was two hours each way when I lived in Winchester, is now one hour each way.

If you cannot work both ideas into one sentence and need to explain your logic:

- My commute to work is now one hour each way, in large part because I am using the Toll Road where I can travel on average about 50 mph. I am also car pooling, which allows us access to the restricted lanes on the Toll Road, using EZ-Pass.

- In contrast, my commute to work when I used Route 7 was two hours each way; in large part because of all the school buses and stop lights. Traffic also moves slower on Route 7 because of all the merging traffic from numerous side streets along this route.

Constructing bullets on the same subject:

If you are providing limited information:

- In 1940, Germany invaded France and, one year later, the Soviet Union.

If you are providing a lot of detail with two data points on the same subject:

- In 1940, Germany invaded France with 42 divisions—including 12 Panzer Divisions commanded by General Guderian—that moved through the Ardennes Forest to attack a lightly defended part of the French border. As a result of this maneuver, Germany cut off hundreds of thousands of French troops, who were positioned to the north across Belgium, from their supply lines.

- One year later, Germany invaded the Soviet Union along three main fronts with the largest army ever assembled, some two million men, 20,000 tanks, and 10,000 artillery pieces. The Germans gave the code name Barbarossa to this operation.

Similarly if you are making comparisons between any X and Y—leader, country, or technical process—and Y is the main focus of the topic sentence, write your bullet points so Y is their main focus. Information on X belongs in a dependent clause, or if the bullet points are long, after the bullet point on Y.

Bullets Points with the Same or Different Subject

If you have two pieces of information with the same subject, write one bullet point unless the information is extensive and combining the information turns the bullet point into a dense word brick.

If your supporting information has different subjects, start a new bullet point with each new subject, unless a commonality exists between the different subjects that is being contrasted with information in a subsequent bullet point. In that case, the bullets should focus on the contrast.

Constructing bullets on different subjects:

Topic Sentence: From 1950 to 1955, economic growth in Europe varied considerably by country.

- The economy in France has soared over the past five years while growth in Italy has also been strong, averaging well over 5 percent per year.

- Britain's economy has posted only modest growth—about 2 percent per year since 1950—and Germany's economy has declined at about 1 percent per year.

Constructing better paragraphs:

The paragraph below is quite choppy because it jumps back and forth between related issues:

Poorly constructed paragraph: This Rocky Mountain fire has grown to become one of the most destructive wildfires in US history. The blaze has already consumed 190,000 acres, destroyed 567 homes, and forced the evacuation of more than 10,000 people. More than **2,000 firefighters** have been committed to fighting the blaze, which is now 90 percent **contained**. A combination of dead and dying trees caused by prolonged drought, high temperatures, low humidity, and rapidly shifting high winds made the fire costly and difficult to contain. Local officials claim the wildfire is likely to be completely contained by this weekend. They estimate the **cost of fighting the fire so far at $50 million.**

The number of firefighters involved and the cost for fighting the fire (in last sentence) are related issues; discuss similar issues in the same place. Pulling together information on the status of containment will improve the paper's flow.

Better paragraph: The Rocky Mountain fire has grown to become one of the most destructive wildfires in US history. The fire has already consumed 190,000 acres, destroyed 567 homes, and forced the evacuation of more than 10,000 people. According to local officials, the blaze is now 90 percent contained and is likely to be completely contained by the end of this weekend. Local officials estimate the cost of fighting the fire so far, in which 2,000 firefighters are involved, at $50 million. A combination of dead and dying trees caused by prolonged drought, high temperatures, low humidity, and rapidly shifting high winds made the fire costly and difficult to contain.

The following is an example of the value of putting information that elaborates on the topic immediately after the issue:

Poorly constructed paragraph: The number of refugees at the refugee camp is rapidly growing as nearly 3,000 people are arriving at the camp daily to escape hunger and fighting. The League of Nations has warned that its life-saving operation is at risk because they have only received about one-tenth of the $10 million they need. **Refugees arrive at the camp weakened and malnourished from their arduous journey, increasing the chance for disease and illness to spread.**

The last sentence elaborates on the condition of the refugees, and is probably a better fit after the first sentence that notes how many refugees are arriving daily.

Better paragraph: The number of refugees at the refugee camp is rapidly growing as nearly 3,000 people are arriving at the camp daily to escape hunger and fighting. Refugees arrive at the camp weakened and malnourished from their arduous journey, increasing the chances for disease and illness to spread. The League of Nations has warned that its life-saving operation is at risk because it only received about one-tenth of the $10 million it needs.

8. Treat Peripheral Information Separately

A simple rule to help you decide whether to create a text box or an appendix is: if the information cannot be characterized as an integral part of one of the major sections of your paper (the *"what?"*, *"why now?"*, *impact so far*, *outlook*, and/or *implications*), it probably belongs in a text box. If you deleted the information in question from the paper, how much of your main message, if any, would be lost?

Another question to ask yourself is whether the amount of space and detail you are devoting to a particular aspect of your paper is consistent with that aspect's relative importance to the section. If you are writing a section on how country X plans to boost economic growth and you have identified three strategies (A, B, and C) in order of decreasing importance, you should not be devoting four paragraphs and a lot of detail to C if you have not given a commensurate amount of space and detail to A and B. The solution often is to put most of the material on C in a text box.

Material that belongs in a text box can be interesting and relevant but can be disruptive to the flow of your paper's key ideas and line of argument if left as part of the main text. Such material often is background material that provides additional explanation or elaboration, details, and context, or may address tangential issues and actors that are not the focus of your paper but may arise in the reader's mind through association with your paper's main focus.

Material that belongs in a text box can be interesting and relevant but can be disruptive to the flow of your paper's key ideas and line of argument.

Typically, information works best in a text box when you are discussing:

Historical information, unless the historical information is directly relevant to a main point in your paper, such as the last three times Country X was faced with this situation, it did Y. Personal information on a leader's education, previous experience, and leadership style usually belongs in a text box if these are peripheral issues in a paper that is focusing on policies and objectives rather than the individual.

Information on how an entity or entities are organized. For example, to whom does the organization report and what subordinate organizations report to it, when and why was it established, and number of personnel. In some papers—such as those examining bureaucratic responsibility for an event, program, or an entity's capabilities—however, information on an entity's organization is directly relevant and would be in the paper's main body. In this case, information on an organization's origin and history probably would still work best in a text box.

Details on sourcing or methodology, especially if the sourcing or methodology is unique and requires explanation, or if it serves as the focal point for your research and analysis. A paper, for example, that was based on a collective review of information found on websites or the print media probably would benefit from a text box providing specific information on which websites and newspapers you researched, characteristics and ownership, and their relative prominence and importance. You might also consider using a text box to discuss your confidence in the paper's key judgments, highlighting your information gaps, the importance of various sources of information, or the potential for deception.[10]

Technical and scientific information, especially if it involves formulas and equations, an elaboration on scientific principles, or even how men once were **drafted by lottery to join the Spanish army**. For example, a paper that examined a country's program to develop multiple re-entry vehicles for its ballistic missile force might include a text box on whatever physical forces are at work that influence where these vehicles land. Some readers might be interested in such a discussion and some might not. Do not use your paper as a platform to demonstrate your technical and scientific expertise if such material falls outside the main interests of your target audience.

[10] See Pherson and Pherson, *Critical Thinking for Strategic Intelligence*, Chapter 9 and 10: Can I Trust the Sources?, Dealing with Deception?, and How Should I Evaluate Sources on the Internet?, pp. 97, 104, and 111.

Comparisons with other countries, groups, themes, and individuals that are peripheral to the main focus of the paper. If your paper's focus is on country X's economic policies and resurgence, information that contrasts country X's economic policies and performance with other countries in the region probably belongs in a text box. Similarly, if the focus of your paper is on the major policy differences and goals of two leading presidential candidates, information on the policy preferences of the lesser candidates probably should be discussed in a text box.

Material for a text box often works as a stand-alone story: you can extract the text box and set it aside and it will hold together in a meaningful way. As a result, the same text box or major elements within a text box may be appropriate for inclusion in multiple papers.

> **Constructing effective text boxes:**
> Text boxes providing background information—dates, impetus, and outcome—of several past conflicts between Bleakistan and Freedonia would be useful in a paper discussing:
> - A recent increase in tension between the countries and the outlook for another round of fighting.
> - Negotiations between the countries to end a long-standing dispute that is largely responsible for the previous conflicts.
> - The current military superiority of one country over the other.

Factors to consider when writing text boxes are their length, placement, and number. If scant material for a text box can be found, you could try to weave this information into a dependent clause or a separate sentence in the main text. When you have more material, the text box is a good fallback.

As a general rule, a text box should not exceed one page. Text boxes that exceed one page start to look like separate papers unto themselves, and an appendix would probably provide a better solution.

Sometimes authors are tempted to throw "everything and the kitchen sink" into a text box because by definition the information in a text box is mostly background or amplifying material. That would be a mistake; the rules of effective writing apply to text boxes and appendices as well as the main text. Text boxes should have a well-defined purpose that serves as a filter for what belongs in them and keeps them from becoming a central repository for less relevant information.

> *Text boxes should have a well-defined purpose that serves as a filter for what belongs in them and keeps them from becoming a central repository for less relevant information.*

If the text box is short, no more than a couple of sentences, the optimal location is immediately after the paragraph that introduces the issue on which the text box is based, even if discussion of this issue in the main body of the paper continues for several more paragraphs after the text box. A short text box, which is more or less just a footnote, is likely to cause minimal disruption in the flow of the paper. A longer text box of several paragraphs, however, is likely to be more disruptive and probably is better placed after the last paragraph that discusses the issue, even if the text box relates mostly to an earlier paragraph in that discussion.

Placing text boxes correctly:

Section of Paper: Factors Driving Economic Growth in Freedonia

Paragraph 1: Foreign investment in copper and aluminum extraction industries

Paragraph 2: Tax credits for construction of large copper and aluminum smelting complexes

Paragraph 3: Increased exports of copper and aluminum

This would be the optimal location for a several-paragraph text box on copper and aluminum reserves, location, history of discovery and development, and foreign investment.

Paragraphs 4 and 5: Government spending

Paragraph 6 and 7: Increased labor productivity

A text box is not optimal here given the likelihood the reader has mentally moved on from copper and aluminum industries by this point in the section.

Longer text boxes that contain more than one paragraph probably should include a title. Unlike the title for the paper, a title for a text box does not necessarily have to be analytic. The number of text boxes should be consistent with the length of the paper or they will seem like a distraction, breaking up the flow of the main analytic message. Similarly, the length of a text box should be in proportion to the length of the main story. If, for example, the main story is three or four paragraphs, a text box that has two or three paragraphs would appear more like another main story rather than a side bar.

Part IV: Refining the Draft

After you have completed your first draft, you are probably about halfway to turning in your paper for review. Go back to the title and begin a comprehensive review of each paragraph's analytic coherence, the organization and flow, conciseness of language, and misspellings and grammatical errors. Even minor mistakes and typographical errors will prompt the reader to question the seriousness of the analysis.

If you make a substantive or organizational change in one part of the paper, probably other parts of the paper will require changes as well. Because of this, review is, at a minimum, a two-stage process. The only way to be confident that a draft holds together is to begin with the first word and read the paper in its entirety.

Conducting a final review of the paper with a hard copy is almost always more effective and efficient; avoid doing substantive reviews exclusively on the computer. Some experienced writers find it useful to read the draft out loud. The key to effective reviewing is to read the draft as the reader and not as the author. Focus on the words in the paper—not what you think you are saying in your head—and do not settle for close enough to what you intended to say. In Part IV, we discuss how to:

Review Paragraphs for Analytic Coherence

Economize on Words

Conduct a Final Review

9. Review Paragraphs for Analytic Coherence

Think of your paper as a puzzle with a message and each paragraph as a piece in this puzzle. For the reader to get this message, all the pieces of the puzzle need to be present, and they need to fit together smoothly. Information in a paragraph that does not belong or belongs in another paragraph throws the reader off track. To get this puzzle right, you will have to be systematic in examining each sentence of each paragraph from several different perspectives.

This chapter is about how to do that in a **step-by-step** fashion that at first is likely to be time-consuming and appear too tedious for you. Over time, however, you will internalize this procedure and the pace at which you begin to insert, delete, or move text around will pick up dramatically.

When matching up and comparing the topic sentence of the paragraph with the supporting information block, four things are possible, only one of which is good:

- All the ideas and information are there and match up perfectly.
- Main ideas in the topic sentence are not addressed in the supporting information.
- Information in the supporting information block is not adequately represented in the topic sentence, and it needs to be.
- Irrelevant information appears in the information block that does not support the main idea(s) in the topic sentence.

Outlined below is a procedure for catching these inconsistencies (see Figure 9). Start by separating the topic sentence with a temporary paragraph break from the remainder of the paragraph.

Figure 9. Reviewing Paragraphs for Analytic Coherence

Use the following six steps when reviewing paragraphs:

1. Read the entire paragraph. Is there material that would better fit in another paragraph?
2. Begin with the topic sentence. Is it analytic, precise, and clear?
3. Separate each sentence in your supporting information block. Does it directly support the main idea(s) in the topic sentence? Or elaborate on a main piece of supporting evidence?
4. Look for information that is irrelevant to the main ideas in the topic sentence. Can you find a home for it?
5. Review your topic sentence again. Are adjustments to the main ideas based on your thorough review of the supporting information?
6. Review your topic sentence one more time. Can you add language that tightens the connection between it and the supporting information?

Step 1. Read the entire paragraph. If there appears to be something amiss in the paragraph, there probably is. Is there material you have read in a previous paragraph that belongs in this paragraph, or material in this paragraph that is a better fit in a previous paragraph?

Step 2. Evaluate your topic sentence. Is it analytic, precise, and clear? If not, underline the sentence or words or phrases that may be problems. At this stage in the paragraph review, evaluating the topic sentence from the perspective of accuracy and completeness is difficult until each sentence in the paragraph has been thoroughly examined.

Step 3. Evaluate your supporting information from the perspective of relevance and support to the main ideas in the topic sentence. The main ideas in your topic sentence are built around primary subject and verb constructions that highlight their importance. Remember that dependent and conditional clauses in your topic sentence typically convey background material that is not the main point and only elaborates on it.

Evaluate each sentence or independent clause separately. If the sentence is a compound sentence, evaluate the clauses separately. Does the sentence or independent clause directly support or link back to the main idea(s) in the topic sentence? If not, three explanations are possible.

- First, you may be asking the reader to read between the lines or to guess. In that case, you need to add language to clarify the relevance or logical connection of the sentence or independent clause to the main idea in the topic sentence.

- Second, the information under review is not directly relevant to the main idea(s) in your topic sentence but instead supports, relates to, or provides context for another sentence that does directly support the topic sentence. A sentence or independent clause that plays this role in the paragraph typically should be placed directly after the sentence it supports or reworked as a dependent or adjectival clause. Move it there or rework it as a dependent clause.

- Third, the information is neither relevant to a main point in the topic sentence nor to a sentence that supports the topic sentence. In that case, underline it.

Evaluating the supporting information in a paragraph:

Main idea for the paragraph: **Market demand for our products typically falls sharply during a period of slow economic growth,** especially if the downturn is preceded by a period of strong economic growth.

Poor approach: **The 1978-80 recession, which was triggered by high oil prices and increased government taxation, occurred after a decade of economic growth that averaged more than 5 percent per year.** Market demand for product A and product B fell 30 and 40 percent, respectively, during that recession.

The first sentence does not directly support the main idea in the topic sentence that demand for Product A and Product B falls sharply during a period of slow economic growth.

A better approach: Market demand for product A and product B fell 30 and 40 percent, respectively, during the 1978-80 recession. **That downturn, which was triggered by high oil prices and increased government taxation, followed a 10-year period of economic growth that averaged more than 5 percent per year.**

The information in the second sentence elaborates on information in the preceding sentence that supports the topic sentence and is best placed after that information.

Sentences in the supporting information block that begin with another subject or discuss an issue unrelated to or inconsistent with the topic sentence are a tip-off that maybe this material is irrelevant, belongs in a dependent clause in a sentence that directly supports the topic sentence, or needs to be reworked and placed after that sentence.

Spotting and fixing irrelevant material:

Incorrect: Joseph Stalin was a brutal dictator. He periodically would grant clemency to a few criminals and loved dogs. Stalin was responsible for the murder of millions of people.

Correct: Joseph Stalin was a brutal dictator. Despite periodically granting clemency to a few criminals and loving dogs, he was responsible for the murder of millions of people.

Remember the two-degrees-of-separation rule: background information that elaborates on other background information that is relevant to information that supports the topic sentence is one degree of separation too far and needs to be deleted.

Invoking the two-degrees-of-separation rule:

Sample Paragraph: Street crime in Rome is skyrocketing, especially by criminal gangs claiming to be Roman soldiers. Roman constables arrested a criminal gang last month whose members were impersonating Roman soldiers and carrying faked documents identifying them as members of the 3rd Roman legion. The documents were forged by Tiberius Mirage, one of the best document forgers in Rome. **Tiberius fled Greece 20 years ago after Athenian police issued a warrant for his arrest and planned to execute him.**

This supporting information in the last sentence can easily be deleted without any harm to the analysis; it qualifies for deletion based on the two degrees of separation rule.

Step 4. Review the supporting information that you have underlined. Can the topic sentence be expanded to account for this information without creating an awkward, difficult-to-read topic sentence? No. Can the information be used as a text box (as discussed in chapter 7)? No. Can the information be used as a stand-alone paragraph after the paragraph in review? No. Move this information to the end of your paper. Do not delete it. You may yet find a place for it.

Step 5. Review your topic sentence again, especially the underlined words or phrases, based on a much clearer sense of your supporting information and its focus. Does it need to be modified to make it more accurate and complete?

Step 6. Can you add subordinate clauses, phrases, or words to the topic sentence (without making it cumbersome and awkward) that help to tie the paragraph even more tightly together?

Using clauses to make a paragraph tighter:

Sample paragraph: Several top military commanders, **including the heads of the Air Force and Navy,** last week switched their loyalty and are now backing a coup, leaving the regime with almost no support among top military officers. A growing perception in the military that the regime has no chance of surviving probably is responsible for the most recent defections.

The highlighted phrase would be a good phrase to add to the topic sentence because it creates an even tighter connection with the supporting information.

- Bullet on Air Force Commander X
- Bullet on Navy Commander Y
- Bullet on two Army division commanders

65

10. Economize on Words

After getting your ideas and information lined up the way you think they make the most sense, it is time to make your text more concise. A natural inclination for many authors is to resist deleting text. You can almost always delete some text. Most of your readers are busy people. They will not want to read one more word than is necessary to understand your point. If you are having difficulty deciding whether a word, phrase, sentence, paragraph, or text box should be deleted, **cut it out**!

Review each sentence looking for language that you can delete without any loss or harm to what you are trying to convey. You can tighten your text by:

- Eliminating redundant language.
- Deleting unnecessary verbiage.
- Deleting unnecessary details that have little or no significance to your target audience.
- Finding alternative language that says the same thing in fewer words.

Delete Redundant Language

The use of different words and a different sentence construction does not mean that the information is not redundant. Remember the reader is processing ideas and information, not words. When comparing or assessing sentences for redundancy, ask yourself what new information is in the sentence that may be redundant. Do not compare words, rather compare ideas and information. Delete the redundant material and save any new information in a shorter second sentence or try to fold the new information into the first sentence.

> **Removing redundant language:**
>
> **Sample sentence:** Without a mission statement, analysts can easily veer off course, add irrelevant material, or end up with analysis that has no clear focus [and is only loosely tied together].
>
> *"Is only loosely tied together" is the definition of unfocused and the phrase can be deleted.*

Review each sentence looking for ideas and phrases within sentences that are repetitive. In some cases, words are redundant because they are implied in the context of other words in the sentence: "blamed on [*the negative consequences of*] the drought" or "a [*government*] delegation led by the prime minister." Another tip-off that you may be able to tighten the language is more than one reference to the same action or subject in the same sentence. You may have to change some language or move text around, but most of the time you will end up with a better flowing sentence.

Eliminating repetition:

Poor sentence: The prisoner John Doe **officially passed** into German custody on 1 October, with a German Army **official confirming** that Doe passed through the Ardennes Forest border crossing between Germany and France, the Berlin Times reported.

Better sentence: A German Army **official confirmed** that the prisoner John Doe on 1 October passed into German custody at the Ardennes Forest border crossing between Germany and France, the Berlin Times reported.

Delete Excess Verbiage

Scrub your text looking for words that add little or nothing to the point you are making. Delete these words. Three prime candidates for deletion from almost every sentence are "very," "also," and "then." You can also delete "in order" from "in order to." Make this a habit. The more you practice this skill, the more automatic the process will become, guaranteed. Most of the time this excess verbiage is found after the main verb and near the end of the sentence in adjective and prepositional clauses. Typically the sentence loses nothing in meaning when this language is deleted because it is already understood.

Trimming excess verbiage:

… prompting the Prime Minister to **[threaten that his country would undertake]** order a rescue operation …

… the granting of an amnesty was **[an unusual act and]** unprecedented.

Do not make your reader **[have to]** work harder than necessary.

Mr. Doe is a tough, experienced diplomat and a formidable negotiator with an impressive command of detail **[on the issues he oversees,]** and **[he possesses]** a sharp and penetrating intellect.

Delete text that is so implicit it is obvious. One of the ways to catch text that states the obvious is to read and mentally process each sentence in your draft from a "no-kidding" perspective. If a sentence elicits a "no-kidding" response, the sentence probably can be deleted with little loss in value to your reader. Apply this litmus test to both factual and analytic sentences.

Applying the "no-kidding" rule:

The incumbent sheriff's reelection campaign is emphasizing crime-will-go-up scare tactics and his opponent's ties to the town's mayor and dog catcher, both of whom are notoriously corrupt and widely unpopular. **[The sheriff's strategy to link his opponent to the mayor and dog catcher is likely intended to sway voters who share a low opinion of both men.]**

The last sentence can easily be deleted.

All of us have our favorite expressions or ways of saying certain things. Unfortunately, some of these pet phrases may be a bit long-winded and provide no substantive value. Make a list of words and phrases that you are prone to use and make a corresponding list of shorter words and phrases. Once you put these words and phrases on a must-delete list, the likelihood that you use them again is small. We use many of these expressions primarily out of habit. Below are a few examples.

Eschewing pet phrases:

The stockholders agreed with the **[thrust of the]** CEO's comment that more money should be spent on R&D.

The firm ABC has sharply increased R&D spending **[for the purpose of]** to accelerate**[ing]** its development of widget X.

Loudoun County is the **[largest]** most populated county in Virginia **[in terms of population]**.

The struggling student was **[taking advantage of]** using the summer break to prepare for the next academic year.

Adjectives and adverbs that modify nouns and verbs that do not need modifying are another target for easy deletions. The nuance that the writer usually ascribes to these words is completely lost on the reader most of the time. The vacuity of these words, which can be masked if only one appears in a sentence, is readily apparent when you insert several of them into a single sentence.

When citing an individual's views on an issue, those comments almost always adequately define the context. They do not need to be prefaced with an introductory phrase that explains the context for the remarks.

Eliminating unnecessary modifiers and phrases:

The regime has [concrete] plans to concede [actual] power to the protestors after several countries put [real] pressure on regime leaders to make [real] political concessions and [effectively] completed preparations to condemn the regime at the UN.

[While discussing the role of the Food Board last week], Agricultural Minister Wilson last week argued the Food Board was necessary to coordinate the position of all the government agencies that regulate the beef industry.

Delete Unnecessary Detail

How much detail to include in your paper is a judgment call. You have to weigh how important the details are against limits you may have on the length of your paper. Details come in at least two varieties: general facts that explain and elaborate, and information that identifies people, places, and things by specific name. In both cases, the litmus test for whether this material survives is how important it is to your reader, so you must understand your audience's needs and interests. In some cases, your audience may be interested in both the general facts and the identifying information and, in other cases, maybe only the general facts. A good question to ask when considering

whether to delete details is: if you cut the information, would it matter to your reader? Would they be grateful you did not force them to read material in which they have little interest? Details that may not matter to your target audience include:

- The venue for a statement if it lacks analytic significance: "The manager of the baseball team [at the ballpark] said …"

- Numerical details that are too exact (unless the precision is important): Freedonia's GDP last year was $214,345,123.23. "About $214 million" probably would suffice.

Discarding details that do not matter:

The Potomac Lakes high school basketball team is likely to win another state championship given the number of returning players from last year's championship squad. Four of the starters from last year are returning, including the center, both forwards, and the point guard. Center Jonathan Taller, who started on both previous championship teams, is considered one of the best players in the county and is a strong academic student. [A number of universities, including Virginia Tech, West Virginia University, Clemson, and UCLA, have already offered him scholarships to play collegiate basketball. His older brother, Mark Taller, played at Virginia Tech during 2004-07.]

Unless you are writing for the local newspaper, your readers might not be interested in the information in the last two sentences.

There are some general guidelines that apply to how much of a person's name to include.

- If the individual is not significant and does not appear in the remainder of the paper, neither the person's first nor last name needs to be included. The person's position is enough information: "A border guard … fired at the tourist."

- If the individual is important or your target audience knows the individual personally, citing the individual's title and full name probably is necessary in the first reference to that individual. After that, the individual's last name probably suffices unless there are multiple persons with the same last name in your paper. In that case, using the person's title and last name is necessary in subsequent references: "Foreign Minister Perez and Interior Minister Perez are long-time political foes."

- With some foreign names, there is a convention to refer to the individual by citing less than the complete name. These conventions vary, and the correct one should be researched and used.

A good question to ask when considering whether to delete details is: if you cut the information, would it matter to your reader? Would they be grateful you did not force them to read material in which they have little interest?

Find Shorter, Alternative Language

Compare back-to-back sentences that refer to the same subject and theme to determine whether the sentences can be combined into a single sentence that has fewer words with only one reference to the same subject and theme. Three situations in which you often can combine sentences or delete phrases are:

- A first sentence that provides only background or context information followed by a second sentence that includes the main action or central point. *Write one sentence by putting the background material in a clause.*

- A first sentence that provides a general characterization of an issue followed by a second sentence that elaborates on that issue. *Write one sentence by folding the characterization into the more specific issue.*

- A second sentence that includes context that is already clear from the first sentence.

Combining sentences for brevity:

Poor sentence construction: The police chief met with the mayor to hear her concerns about the impact of crime on the city's economy. After the meeting, the police chief announced that he would increase police patrols throughout the city and establish a hotline for reporting suspicious activity.

Better sentence construction: After meeting with the mayor to hear her concerns about the impact of crime on the city's economy, the police chief announced that he would increase police patrols throughout the city and establish a hotline for reporting suspicious activity.

Use verbs rather than prepositional phrases and other constructions. Generally speaking, verb phrases are shorter, and because they are more direct, are easier to read. Verb phrases are not going to save a lot of text, but they make for a crisper sentence. Replace roundabout language with shorter alternatives. Roundabout language can often involve a verb linked to a prepositional clause that is essentially the definition of a single verb. Use the single verb.

Using verbs to make sentences shorter:

… would work with Bleakistan **[in the development of]** to develop its defense industry.

… which prompted King Arthur**['s pardon of]** to pardon six horse thieves in December.

… the team was asked to **[perform an analysis of]** analyze the samples.

Reporters **[searched for deeper meaning of]** contemplated the trial's potential impact on society and the criminal justice system.

11. Conduct a Final Review

All good writers know they are not finished when the draft is completed. Before a paper is submitted, it must also undergo a substantive review and self-editing. Your credibility rests on being able to catch gaps in logic, errors in fact, errors in analysis, misspellings, and grammatical mistakes.[11] Good writers take pride in delivering a polished product to their editors and reviewers.

Start your self-edit with the title. The first and last thing your target audience may read is the title. Does the title capture the *"what?"* and *"so what?"* of your analytic message? Is it direct and to the point? If the title resonates with your target audience and piques their interest, they will begin to read the paper. If it does not, they may not read the first sentence. Can you shorten the title? One approach is to look for shorter variants for key words and ideas in the title and words that do not add much value.

Shortening titles:

Title: Significant Local Opposition to Extremists in Antarctica
Shorter variant: Residents Oppose Extremists in Antarctica

Title: Major Alaskan Campaign to Influence Elections in Antarctica Underway
Shorter variant: Alaska Seeking to Sway Voters in Antarctica

Title: Increased Spending on Advertising Expanding Market Potential for Widget Sales
Shorter variant: Increased Advertising Improving Prospects for Widget Sales

---

Read through the paper just looking at the topic sentences. Does the analytic storyline progress with each and every topic sentence? Getting your target audience to read your paper with an effective title is only the first step. They can stop reading at any time. Topic sentences that advance the storyline will keep your readers engaged. Make sure the judgments in your topic sentence are supported by sufficient reasoning and compelling evidence. Is this reasoning and evidence laid out clearly? Review your paragraphs again for analytic coherence.

Review the order of presentation in each paragraph. Is the order optimal? Does the paragraph maintain a parallel structure in the presentation of like issues throughout the paragraph or does it whipsaw back and forth? Is your most compelling evidence presented first? Do some paragraphs look like word bricks or have so many bullets they look like a grocery list? Are there unnecessary details in the paragraph?

Consider whether any terms need to be explained or whether any background or context should be added. Is this information in the optimal place in the draft for your reader, i.e., at or soon after a potential question may arise? For readers to understand your analytic judgments and how the pieces of the puzzle fit together, they must understand the pieces of the puzzle. Knowing your audience is necessary for making good decisions about how much background explanation and context you need to include.

Always do a spelling and grammar check and review a printed copy of the draft before you turn in your draft for review or send it out for coordination (see Figure 10).

---

[11] Detailed checklists for reviewing a draft can be found in Pherson and Pherson, *Critical Thinking for Strategic Intelligence*, Chapter 20: How Do I Know When I Am Finished?, p. 225.

Figure 10. Five Common Grammatical Errors

1. **Misuse of relative pronouns.** A relative pronoun "relates" a subordinate clause to the rest of a sentence: who, whom, that, which.
   - Who/whom. **Whom** is always an objective pronoun; **who** is the subjective.
   - That/which. **That** is used with restrictive clauses, and **which** with non-restrictive clauses that are set off with commas.

   Correct Examples: From whom did you get the recipe? I selected the lettuce that had the least wilted leaves. He made the salad, which did not taste quite right.

2. **Lack of subject-verb agreement.** Singular subjects need singular verbs, and plural subjects require plural verbs.

   Correct Example: Does anyone in this room claim responsibility for this error?

3. **Disagreement between pronouns and their antecedents.** A pronoun must agree in person, number, and gender with the word, phrase, or clause to which it refers.

   Correct Example: If a person wants to succeed professionally, he or she must know the rules of the game.

4. **Confusing possessive pronouns and contracted pronouns.** A possessive pronoun substitutes for a possessive noun: his, hers, yours, its, ours, theirs, and whose. A contracted pronoun is a shortened version of a pronoun plus the verb "is". It's = it is, who's = who is. Avoid contractions in analytic writing.

   Correct Example: I do not know whose car that is, but it is in my parking space.

5. **Using "however" incorrectly.** "However" should not be used to link two independent clauses; it is an adverb, not a conjunction. Its proper purpose is to contrast two independent clauses.

   Correct example: Bill, however, was not able to understand the problem.

   The use of "however" here presumes that there were others who did understand the problem.

   Incorrect example: I wanted to be on the conference panel, <u>however</u>, by the time I applied the deadline had passed.

   Correct example: I wanted to be on the conference panel; <u>however</u>, by the time I applied the deadline had passed.

   Correct alternative construction: I wanted to be on the conference panel, <u>but</u> by the time I applied the deadline had passed.

   Correct alternative construction: <u>Although</u> I wanted to be on the conference panel, by the time I applied the deadline had passed.

You will rue the day you did not make this a habit! Submitting a product with spelling or grammar mistakes will mark you as a sloppy thinker no matter how brilliant your analysis. Do not rely on a word-processing spell checker, which can miss some egregious errors (see Figure 11).

Ideally, you should take a break and focus your mind on something else before going back to review and self-edit your product. Simply distancing yourself from your writing, even for a short period of time, will help you catch errors you might otherwise have missed.

Always do a spelling and grammar check and review a printed hard copy of the draft before you turn in your draft for review.

If you are not sure of a word's meaning, refer to the dictionary. Do not take the risk that your understanding of the word is correct. Many words that are similar in spelling have much different meanings, such as: capability and capacity, principal and principle, affect and effect, capital and capitol, to name just a few.

Figure 11. Published Errors that Spell Check Missed

The following errors were missed by spell check in papers the authors wrote and reviewed electronically and were only caught when we reviewed the paper in hard copy:

- "This material **compliments** our publication." *Should be "complements."*
- "The NGA **Collage** offers courses in analytical thinking and writing." *Should be "College."*
- "Ms. Angela Smith gave a lecture at noon yesterday. **He** spoke about national security issues." *Should be "she," since Ms. Smith is a woman.*
- "Our intent is to make the base as difficult a target **us** possible." *Should be "as."*
- "Unfortunately the **brake** in action was not accounted for in the report." *Should be "break."*
- "He requested **a** article on the topic." *Should be "an article."*
- "To maintain the **qualify** of your report, it is essential to review your writing." *Should be "quality."*
- "Does the military have the **capacity** to secure the border?" *Should be "capability."*
- "The report **derails** the intelligence gathered by our top analysts." *Should be "details."*
- "The **carnal** model will provide the analyst with different versions of the relationships between the various variables." *Should be "causal."*
- "To rise **about** our limited perspective, analysts must first ground themselves in the forces and personalities driving the situation." *Should be "above."*

Some "small" errors can make the analysis look like nonsense, for example, if an analyst inadvertently inserts Pakistan rather than Afghanistan as the noun in a sentence. Such errors are not difficult to make if you are working on a paper in which Afghanistan and Pakistan both feature prominently. The mind often sees what it expects to see even when that something is not there. The same mental bias can cause you to miss typographical and spelling errors.

Having a colleague review your draft is a great way to catch errors that you may not find because of your familiarity with the text. The more important the topic and the more widely it will be distributed, the more critical it is to have someone review your draft no matter how serious the time constraints (see Figure 12). Your colleagues are not going to be as familiar with the text as you are and will have to rely on the words alone. How hard did they have to think to process the main analytic judgments and the basis for them? Would you attribute any problems they encountered to the concepts or the language?

Make sure the judgments in your topic sentence are supported by sufficient reasoning and compelling evidence.

Although well-written and well-supported arguments will keep your reader reading, establishing credibility with your target audience is the key to getting your reader to accept your analytic message. The most effective way to establish credibility is to demonstrate that you have thoroughly reviewed all the relevant information and objectively considered other alternatives.

Before delivering your product for review, ask yourself the 14 questions in the Analytic Writer's Checklist (see inside front cover). If you can answer each question with confidence, you are well on your way to becoming a polished writer. Reviewers will look forward to receiving your drafts and return them quickly.

Figure 12. Tips for How to Rite Rite

- Don't abbrev.
- Check to see if you any words out.
- Be carefully to use adjectives and adverbs correct.
- About sentence fragments.
- Always avoid alliteration.
- Prepositions are not words to end sentences with.
- Avoid clichés like the plague.
- Employ the vernacular.
- Eschew ampersands & abbreviations, etc.
- Parenthetical remarks (however relevant) are unnecessary.
- It is wrong ever to split an infinitive.
- Contractions aren't proper.
- Foreign words and phrases are not apropos.
- One should never generalize.
- Eliminate quotations. As Ralph Waldo Emerson once said: "I hate quotations. Tell me what you know."
- Comparisons are as bad as clichés.
- Don't be redundant; don't use more words than necessary; it's highly superfluous.
- Profanity sucks.
- Be more or less specific.
- Understatement is always best.
- Exaggeration is a billion times worse than understatement.
- One-word sentences? Eliminate.
- Analogies in writing are like feathers on a snake.
- The passive voice is to be avoided.
- Go around the barn at high noon to avoid colloquialisms.
- Even if a mixed metaphor sings, it should be derailed.
- Who needs rhetorical questions?
- When dangling, don't use participles.
- Don't use no double negatives.
- Each pronoun agrees with their antecedent.
- Just between you and I, case is important.
- Join clauses good, like a conjunction should.
- Don't use commas, that aren't necessary.
- It's important to use apostrophe's right.
- It's better not to unnecessarily split an infinitive.
- Never leave a transitive verb just lay there without an object.
- Only Proper Nouns should be capitalized. also a sentence should begin with a capital and end with a period
- Use hyphens in compound-words, not just in any two-word phrase.
- In letters compositions reports and things like that we use commas to keep a string of items apart.
- Watch out for irregular verbs which have creeped into our language.
- Verbs has to agree with their subject.
- Avoid unnecessary redundancy.
- A writer mustn't shift your point of view.
- Don't write a run-on sentence you've got to punctuate it.

- Author Unknown

Glossaries

Commonly Used Terms
Proofreading Symbols
Recommended Readings

Commonly Used Terms

Word or Phrase	Meaning
Accuracy requirement for a topic sentence	The judgment in the topic sentence summarizes or captures correctly the essence of the supporting information. The analytic judgment is in sync with a reasonable interpretation of the supporting information: the analytic judgment is not saying one thing while the supporting information is saying another.
Active voice	When the actor or subject performs the action of the verb. Active voice constructions eliminate potential ambiguity and are typically more concise.
AIMS process	The audience, issue or intelligence question, message, and storyline for a paper.
Analytic coherance of a paragraph	All the information needed to understand the relevance of the supporting information to the topic sentence is included in the paragraph. None of the information is unnecessary or irrelevant.
Analytic progression	A key requirement for an analytic paper to move the analysis logically and progressively from one section to another and from one paragraph to another without detours or repetition.
Background noise	Contextual and explanatory information in the topic sentence that is not necessary to understand the analytic judgment but takes the emphasis off the judgment. This information often can be placed easily in other sentences in the paragraph.
Bridging sentence	A second sentence that elaborates on the main idea in the paragraph's first sentence by providing additional details or extends the analysis to include a new idea or analytic thrust for the paragraph. Use it to avoid writing a long or cumbersome topic sentence.
Bullet point	Information or evidence used to support or expand on the initial sentence that is indented and set off by a series of black dots or other symbols.
Clarity requirement for a topic sentence	Straightforward and direct language that is grammatically correct and focuses on the main point while minimizing the amount of background material.
Comparison confusion	Contrasting information is not readily apparent, often because the contrast is not stated or the comparison is between "apples" and "oranges."
Completeness requirement for a topic sentence	The topic sentence summarizes completely the main points inferred by the supporting information. If, for example, the supporting information identifies two key factors driving a development, both factors are noted in the topic sentence.

Word or Phrase	Meaning
Digestibility	The reader must be able to readily assimilate the main idea in a topic sentence. If the paper contains too much nonessential background information or the main idea cannot be summarized in one sentence, the topic sentence is too long and the reader will lose focus.
Impact so far section	The impact the development that is the focus of the paper already has had. This section generally is found in papers whose impact is an intermediate result that sets the stage for future developments of a qualitatively different nature.
Implications section	What the development or discovery that is the initial focus of the paper means for your target audience's interests and their decisionmaking. This section often will identify opportunities and dangers as well as what leverage the target audience can bring to bear to prompt or prevent others from acting.
Information roadblock	When the reader becomes lost because of apparent inconsistencies, unexplained linkages, ambiguous references, or unwarranted assumptions about the reader's knowledge of the issue.
Inverted triangle	A graphic that mirrors how a paper is organized, reflecting the amount of space each section takes up and then illustrating how this order can be inverted to contrast a data-driven organization of a paper with a message-driven approach.
Likelihood swings	The probability attached to the same analytic judgment is not consistent throughout the paper.
Mission statement	A sentence that identifies the target audience for the paper and the development or discovery that is important to them as well as how it may affect or serve their interests. The mission statement provides the initial focus for drafting the paper but does not preclude additional research and the refinement of the paper's conclusions.
No-kidding rule	A litmus test for determining if a sentence or phrase can be deleted with little loss of value for the reader.
Numbers gridlock	The reader cannot sort through the numbers presented and make them add up. This problem can occur because different types of numbers are cited in different places in the paper, and this is not made explicit or discrepancies in the data are not acknowledged.

Word or Phrase	Meaning
Two-degrees-of-separation rule	Only one additional sentence provides context or background to support the initial sentence in a bullet point. More than one sentence veers the reader off course from the main judgment.
Outlook section	What is likely to happen next. This section involves significant uncertainty, and a discussion of multiple outcomes may be necessary. Almost every outcome section should identify the most important variables or drivers in determining the outcome. This section may also include indicators that are potential markers of a certain outlook coming to pass.
Parallel presentation	Maintaining the same order in the discussion of issues that is consistent with the previous order in which the issues are presented in the subheads or topic sentence.
Passive voice	When the actor is absent or is the object of the action specified by the verb. Passive voice constructions are less precise and use more words than active sentence voice constructions.
Peripheral information	Information that is not integral to the main issue in the paper but provides additional context or background information. This material, which may include methodological, historical, and/or explanatory information, often fits better in a text box or annex.
Precision requirement for a topic sentence	The judgment in the analytic topic sentence is not ambiguous or open to multiple interpretations. The topic sentence does not hint at the main judgment but states it explicitly.
Pre-drafting litmus test	The ability to clearly and meaningfully state out loud the paper's bottom line before drafting. Any attempt to write a paper without a clear sense of the paper's focus and direction is likely to produce a meandering paper with no central message.
Side bar	A sentence fragment or full sentence that is placed off to the side in a one-column format that highlights a key finding in the article.
So what?	The explanation of why a reader needs to know something.
So what of the so what?	The secondary and tertiary impact of a development and what the reader might want to consider doing next.
Supporting information block	The information and argument in the paragraph that supports the judgment in the topic sentence. The topic sentence and the supporting information block should mesh like cogs in two precisely machined gears.

Word or Phrase	Meaning
Target audience	The group of readers for whom the paper is written.
Text box	A section in a paper that is not integral to the main story but provides additional explanatory or contextual material. A text box is sometimes called a tone box if the background in the box is shaded.
Topic sentence	The first sentence in an analytic paragraph that states the paragraph's main analytic judgment. The topic sentence typically also includes the author's confidence and basis for the judgment.
Unexplained linkages	The information is missing for the reader to relate the significance of the supporting information in the paragraph to the main judgment in the topic sentence.
"What?" section	What has recently changed or has been discovered that is of interest to the paper's target audience. This section is often the first section in an analytic paper or report.
"Why now?" section	Identification and explanation of the factors driving the event or discovery that is the focus of the "what?" section. Before your target readers can improve the situation to take advantage of a potential opportunity, they must thoroughly understand the forces and factors underlying the "what?".

Proofreading Symbols

Meaning	Symbol	Example
Align	‖ or =	• item 1 • item 2
Apostrophe	V	An apostrophe in a persons name denotes possession.
Capitalize	≡	Capitalize organizations such as <u>nato</u>.
Center	⊐ ⊏	⊐ Center this text. ⊏
Close Up	◡	Write as o ne word.
Colon	⩒	There are three items nuts, bolts, and nails.
Comma	⋀	First use a comma to set off an introductory element paranthetical elements or lists.
Delete	℘	Remove this extra word.
Delete and close up	℘	Write as oøne word.
Em dash	$\frac{1}{M}$	A dash if done right can offset important lists.
En dash	$\frac{1}{N}$	The years 1995 98
Flush left	⌐	Flush left.
Flush Right	¬	Flush right.
Hyphen	–/	words like eye-/opener should be hyphenated.
Insert	⋀	Insert here. one word
Let stand	STET	Do not make this change.
Lowercase	ⓛⓒ	Capitalize proper nouns like Dr. Joe, but not regular nouns like Doctor.
Move left	⊏	move to the left.
Move right	⊐	move to the right.

Meaning	Symbol	Example
Move to new position	⟳→	Sometimes a phrase makes ← it is moved earlier more sense when.
New paragraph	¶	Start a new paragraph after this sentence. It will help break up word bricks. ¶
Period	⊙	This sentence is missing a period⊙
Remove paragraph break	no¶	If sentences support the original topic sentences. no ¶ Then join the two short paragraphs.
Run in with previous line	⌐⌐	Run text in with ⌐ text on next line.
Semicolon	⩘	Semicolons help break up lists of people, and their titles, such as: John Doe, president Jane Smith, vice president and Joe Schmo, treasurer.
Set in bold	bf	Use bold sparingly in your paper. bf
Set in italics	ital	Use italics for book titles, such as: Analytic Writing Guide. ital
Set in roman	rom	Use roman when italicized or bolded text should appear as regular text. rom
Space	⧓	Sometimes words need more space between them.
Start a new line	⌐_	If you want to break up a word brick into two paragraphs, then use the "start a new line" symbol. It will help the flow of your paper.
Spell out	sp	Certain measurements like 2 hrs should be spelled out. sp
Subscript	∨	123
Superscript	∧	123
Transpose	∩	Put words in the order correct
Wrong font	wf	This can include incorrect point size or typeface. wf

Recommended Readings

Beebe, Sarah Miller, and Randolph H. Pherson. *Cases in Intelligence Analysis: Structured Analytic Techniques in Action*. Washington, DC: CQ Press, 2012.

Booth, Wayne C., Gregory G. Colomb, and Joseph M. Williams. *The Craft of Research*. 3rd ed. Chicago: University of Chicago Press, 2008.

Chastain, Emma. *How to Write: A Concise Guide to Grammar, Usage & Style (SparkNotes Ultimate Style)*. New York: Spark Publishing, 2005.

Fine, Edith H. and Judith P. Josephson. *Nitty-Gritty Grammar: A Not-So-Serious Guide to Clear Communication*. Berkeley: Ten Speed Press, 1998.

Heuer, Richards J., Jr., and Randolph H. Pherson. *Structured Analytic Techniques for Intelligence Analysis*. Washington, DC: CQ Press, 2011.

Higgins, James M. *101 Creative Problem Solving Techniques: The Handbook of New Ideas for Business*. Writer Park, Florida: The New Management Publishing Company, 1994.

Koegel, Timothy J. *The Exceptional Presenter: A Proven Formula to Open Up and Own the Room*. Expanded ed. Austin, TX, 2007.

Mayberry, Katherine J. *Everyday Arguments: A Guide to Writing and Reading Effective Arguments*. 3rd ed. Boston: Houghton Mifflin, 2009.

Michael Michalko. *Thinkertoys*. 2nd ed. Berkeley: Ten Speed Press, 2006.

Pherson, Katherine Hibbs and Randolph H. Pherson, *Critical Thinking for Strategic Intelligence*. Washington, DC: CQ Press/SAGE Publications, 2013.

Pherson, Randolph H. *Handbook of Analytic Tools and Techniques*. Reston, VA: Pherson Associates, LLC, 2008.

Pink, Daniel H. *A Whole New Mind: Why Right-Brainers Will Rule the Future*. New York: Riverhead Books, 2006.

Roam, Dan. *The Back of the Napkin: Solving Problems and Selling Ideas with Pictures*. Expanded ed. London: The Penguin Group, 2009.

Root-Bernstein, Robert and Michele. *Sparks of Genius: The 13 Thinking Tools of the World's Most Creative People*. Boston: Houghton Mifflin, 1999.

Schum, David A. *The Evidential Foundations of Probabilistic Reasoning*. Evanston, IL: Northwestern University Press, 2001.

Strunk Jr., William and E.B. White. *The Elements of Style*. 50th Anniversary ed. New York: Pearson Education, 2009.

Williams, Joseph M., and Gregory G. Colomb. *Style: Lessons in Clarity and Grace*. 10th ed. New York: Longman, 2010.

US Government Publications

Directorate of Intelligence. *Style Manual & Writers Guide for Intelligence Publications*. 8th ed. Washington DC: Central Intelligence Agency, 2011.

ODNI. *Intelligence Community Directive 203: Analytic Standards*, June 17, 2007, www.dni.gov/electronic_reading_room/ICD_203.pdf.

ODNI. *Intelligence Community Directive 206: Sourcing Requirements for Disseminated Analytic Products*, October 17, 2007, www.dni.gov/electronic_reading_room/ICD_206.pdf.

ODNI. *Intelligence Community Directive 208: Writing for Maximum Utility*, December 18, 2008, www.dni.gov/electronic_reading_room/ICD_208.pdf.

Notes

Notes

Notes

Testimonials from students taking workshops based on the Analytic Writing Guide:

"I learned so much about how to convey analysis effectively and compellingly. My team leader said the draft I wrote after your course was the best since I joined the team."

"In every other class I have taken, the instructors emphasized the importance of good topic sentences, but this class taught me HOW to actually do it."

"The workshop helped me craft better analytic topic sentences using a straightforward and practical approach."

"The workshop provided specific guidance and specific examples that will help me organize a paper I am working on."

Comments from analysts at the Washington/Baltimore High Intensity Drug Trafficking Area Investigative Support Center who reviewed the Analytic Writing Guide:

"The Analytic Writing Guide will be a great resource for new analysts just entering the field of strategic intelligence and a good refresher for experienced analysts. Kaiser and Pherson give sound writing advice—for example, by listing words to avoid using, by explaining how to use verbs to shorten sentences, and by providing questions to ask yourself as you write. It tells the reader how to convey analysis in a concise and thoughtful manner. Overall, it is well written and thorough."